Why Study Linguistics

Why Study Linguistics is designed to help anyone with an interest in studying language understand what linguistics is, and what linguists do. Exploring how the scientific study of language differs from other ways of investigating this uniquely human behavior, *Why Study Linguistics*:

- explores the various topics that students of linguistics study, including sound systems of language, the structure of words and sentences and their meanings, and the wider social context of language change and language variation;
- explains what you might do with a degree in linguistics and the kinds of jobs and careers that studying linguistics prepares you for;
- is supported by a list of links to additional resources available online.

This book is the first of its kind and will be essential reading for anyone considering a course of study in this fascinating subject, as well as teachers, advisors, student mentors, and anyone who wants to know more about the scientific study of language.

Kristin Denham is Professor of Linguistics at Western Washington University, USA.

Anne Lobeck is Professor of Linguistics at Western Washington University, USA.

Routledge Guides to Linguistics

Routledge Guides to Linguistics are a set of concise and accessible guidebooks which provide an overview of the fundamental principles of a subject area in a jargon-free and undaunting format. Designed for students of linguistics who are approaching a particular topic for the first time, or students who are considering studying linguistics and are eager to find out more about it, these books will both introduce the essentials of a subject and provide an ideal springboard for further study.

This series is published in conjunction with the Linguistic Society of America. Founded in 1924 to advance the scientific study of language, the LSA plays a critical role in supporting and disseminating linguistic scholarship both to professional linguists and to the general public.

Series Editor

Betty J. Birner is a Professor of Linguistics and Cognitive Science in the Department of English at Northern Illinois University, USA.

Titles in this series:

Language in Children
Eve V. Clark

Is English Changing?
Steve Kleinedler

Language and Meaning
Betty J. Birner

Why Study Linguistics
Kristin Denham and Anne Lobeck

More information about this series can be found at www.routledge.com/series/RGL

Why Study Linguistics

Kristin Denham and
Anne Lobeck

Taylor & Francis Group

LONDON AND NEW YORK

First published 2019
by Routledge
2 Park Square, Milton Park, Abingdon, Oxon OX14 4RN

and by Routledge
711 Third Avenue, New York, NY 10017

Routledge is an imprint of the Taylor & Francis Group, an informa business

© 2019 Kristin Denham and Anne Lobeck

The right of Kristin Denham and Anne Lobeck to be identified as authors of this work has been asserted by them in accordance with sections 77 and 78 of the Copyright, Designs and Patents Act 1988.

All rights reserved. No part of this book may be reprinted or reproduced or utilised in any form or by any electronic, mechanical, or other means, now known or hereafter invented, including photocopying and recording, or in any information storage or retrieval system, without permission in writing from the publishers.

Trademark notice: Product or corporate names may be trademarks or registered trademarks, and are used only for identification and explanation without intent to infringe.

British Library Cataloguing-in-Publication Data
A catalogue record for this book is available from the British Library

Library of Congress Cataloging-in-Publication Data
A catalog record has been requested for this book

ISBN: 978-1-138-92587-8 (hbk)
ISBN: 978-1-138-92588-5 (pbk)
ISBN: 978-0-429-44462-3 (ebk)

Typeset in Times New Roman
by Out of House Publishing

Visit the eResources: www.routledge.com/9781138925885

Printed and bound in Great Britain by
TJ International Ltd, Padstow, Cornwall

Contents

Acknowledgements x

1 Why read this book? 1
Introduction to the book 1
Who this book is for 1
How to use this book 2

2 Questions linguists ask 5
What is linguistics? 5
   What is language? 6
   Human language versus other animal communication systems 6
   Hockett's design features of language 7
What is a language? 9
   Language variation: languages and dialects 9
   Language change 12
What does it mean to know a language? 16
   Our linguistic intuitions 16
   Linguistic competence and linguistic performance 19
What is grammar? 20
   Our knowledge of grammar 20
   Prescriptive and descriptive grammar 27
   Universal Grammar 30

First language acquisition 31
   Christopher the linguistic savant 32
   Contact languages and language genesis 33
  How do we study language scientifically? 36
   Gathering and analyzing data: the scientific method 37
   An example of scientific inquiry: english wh-question formation 38
   Exploring data from other languages 43

3   The study of sound: phonetics and phonology · 48

Articulatory phonetics 48
Phonological rules 52
Auditory phonetics 54
Allophones and phonemes 54
Syllables 56
Stress 60
Tone and intonation 61
Why study sound? 62

4   The study of words: morphology · 64

Morphemes 65
Derivational and inflectional affixation 66
   Expanding inflectional morphology 68
Word trees 72
Types of categories 76
Morphological typologies 79
What is a word? 81
Why study words? 82

5   The study of sentence structure: syntax · 85

Revisiting syntactic categories 85
Phrase structure 87
Hierarchical structure and recursion 89
Syntactic ambiguity 91

Syntactic typologies 92
Movement 95
Deletion 98
Morphosyntax 99
Why study sentence structure? 102

6 The study of meaning: semantics and pragmatics 104

Semantic relationships among words 104
    Metaphor and figurative language 105
Semantic relationships among sentences 107
How sound and structure influence meaning 108
How context shapes meaning: pragmatics 111
    Maxims of conversation 112
    Presupposition 115
    Politeness 116
    Speech acts 117
Why study meaning? 118

7 Studying language change: historical linguistics 121

The study of language in the eighteenth century 121
The comparative method and language family trees 122
    Proto-Indo-European 125
    Other language families 127
Types of language change 128
    Morphological change 129
    Phonological change (sound change) 130
    Semantic change 131
    Syntactic change 131
Why languages change 133
    Natural processes of language change 133
    Language acquisition 134

Language contact 134
Social identity 135
Why study language change? 135

8 Studying language variation: sociolinguistics 138

Language variation and region 139
Dialectology and lexical variation 140
Phonological variation 142
    Factors affecting sound variation 143
Morphological variation 145
Syntactic variation 146
Language attitudes and linguistic discrimination 147
Language policy and planning 151
Why study language variation? 153

9 Studying language in the brain: psycholinguistics 155

First language acquisition 155
    Language acquisition rules and strategies 158
    What kids' 'mistakes' tell us 160
    Studying language acquisition and syntax 161
Psycholinguistics and Idioma de Señas de Nicaragua 162
Brain lateralization and language functions 164
Aphasia and localization 166
Factors affecting language in the brain 169
Experimental methodologies 170
Sentence processing 172
Why study psycholinguistics? 175

10 After studying linguistics 178

Careers in education 179
    Linguistics professor at a college or university 181
    K12 education 183
    Teaching English to Speakers of Other Languages (TESOL) 186

Testing agencies 188
Non-profits 190
Speech language pathologist 191
Editing and publishing, journalism 193
Lexicography 195
Tech industry 196
Marketing and advertising 198
Language documentation and revitalization 200
Forensic linguistics 202
Polyglot jobs 203
Lots of other things! 206

Index 210

Acknowledgements

We are grateful to have had the opportunity to write this book, and to support the LSA-Routledge book series. Many thanks to Monica Macaulay and Kristen Syrett, authors of the original LSA *Why Major in Linguistics* pamphlet and web page. Their work provided us with an excellent starting point for this project. Thanks also to series editor Betty Birner, for her excellent feedback and support. We are also very grateful to the editors at Routledge who have guided us along the way: Helen Tredgett, Nadia Seemungal, Francesca McGowan, and Elizabeth Cox. Our Western Washington University colleagues Shannon Dubenion-Smith, Jennifer Green, and Edward Vajda have been invaluable resources as well; we are very fortunate to be part of such a vibrant and collegial community of linguists. Thanks to Hugh Conroy for last-minute graphics, to Russell Hugo for image creation, and to WWU student Zoe Buchli for her work on the references. Finally, we thank all of our students, who have taught us how to make linguistics accessible to everyone in a way that we hope informs this book.

1
Why read this book?

Introduction to the book

We assume that if you have picked up this book, you are interested in studying language, and you are probably wondering what exactly linguistics is, and what it is that linguists do. You also might be wondering what kinds of topics students of linguistics explore and learn about. You might also be wondering: What might you do with a degree in linguistics? What kinds of jobs and careers does studying linguistics prepare you for? Although we will not be able to tell you (even if we could) everything there is to know about studying linguistics in this short book, we will provide you with an overview of possible answers to these questions, and direct you to where you might find more information if you wish.

Who this book is for

This book is for students who have—or think they might have—an interest in linguistics. It's also designed to be used by Linguistics program/department faculty and advisors, career center coordinators, librarians, and others to help guide undergraduates with an interest in linguistics. The information presented here can help students decide if they want to major in or study linguistics but it can also be useful for those just wanting to know a little more about the study of language.

How to use this book

This book is organized to provide readers with general information, but also with more detail should readers want to explore the topics covered in more depth. The book has ten chapters, and each of the remaining nine is outlined below. Readers can either read the book cover to cover, or pick and choose the area(s) of most interest to them. Each chapter addresses current topics of research in each area, and also provides some ideas of what we learn from such research about not only language structure, but about language change, variation, and acquisition. Each chapter concludes with a set of key concepts that guide research in these fields, and highlights the knowledge and skills gained by studying each area. We also highlight some of the ways in which the study of each component of grammar can be applied beyond the classroom.

Throughout the book we discuss language change, variation, and acquisition, and we also devote one chapter to each of these areas of study in linguistics.

In **Chapter 2**, *Questions linguists ask*, we provide an overview of the basic questions that linguists seek to answer, and of the fundamental concepts and terminology central to linguistic inquiry. We begin with how linguist Noam Chomsky's ideas have revolutionized the study of language, in particular by considering language as an object of scientific inquiry. We discuss how human language differs from the communication systems of other species, and how language varies over time and space. We discuss what it means to know a language, and how we study and describe our intuitive knowledge of language. We clarify what linguists mean when they talk about 'grammar,' and how an approach to grammar through inquiry differs from other possibly more familiar ways to study language. In this chapter we touch on the study of language variation, language change, and language acquisition, and we also introduce the study of language and the brain. The information we provide in this chapter is introductory, and we elaborate on the topics introduced here in more depth in later chapters.

In **Chapters 3–6** we explore in some depth the study of the components of grammar, providing examples of the phenomena that linguists study, and what such study reveals about the way languages work. Each chapter stands by itself, and readers may read them sequentially or out of order, and may choose to read one or another but not all. In **Chapter 3**, *The study of sound: Phonetics and phonology*, we introduce different ways that linguists study the sounds of language (articulatory and auditory phonetics), and some of the concepts central to the study of phonology (allophones and phonemes, syllable structure, stress, tone and intonation). In **Chapter 4**, *The study of words: Morphology*, we introduce basic word structure (morphemes, affixation, lexical and functional categories of words, word formation rules), and show how words have a structure that can be graphically represented with word tree diagrams. We discuss how languages can be divided into different morphological typologies (analytic, synthetic, polysynthetic), which show us that the definition of 'word' is actually much more complex than it might appear. In **Chapter 5**, *The study of sentence structure: Syntax*, we investigate the fundamentals of sentence structure (phrase structure), including how it can be represented with tree diagrams. We show how we can account for different word orders among languages, and how, even though languages may seem to be syntactically very different, they actually share certain basic syntactic structures. In **Chapter 6**, *The study of meaning: Semantics and pragmatics*, we turn to the study of semantics—word meaning (antonymy, synonymy, polysemy, and other relationships) and sentence meaning (ambiguity, paraphrase, entailment). We discuss how semantics overlaps with syntax (thematic roles, selectional restrictions). In the section on pragmatics we discuss how we derive meaning from context in conversations (maxims of conversation, speech acts) and what it means to threaten, apologize, promise, and regret.

In **Chapter 7**, *Studying language change*, we discuss ways in which linguists study how and why languages change over time, with a focus on the history of English, from Old English to Present Day English. We provide examples of the different aspects of language change (phonological, morphological, syntactic, and semantic), and explore some of the factors that trigger language change. In **Chapter 8**, *Studying language variation: Language in society*, we discuss language variation across different regions (dialect variation), and provide examples of different kinds of language variation (phonological, morphological, syntactic, and semantic) and the linguistic, social, and cultural factors that can lead to variation. We explore how language shapes our identities and our attitudes about ourselves and others. In **Chapter 9**, *Studying psycholinguistics: Language in the brain*, we discuss what research on child language acquisition, studies of language and the brain, studies on how we process language and more tell us about our biological capacity for language.

In **Chapter 10**, *After studying linguistics*, we discuss a number of different ways that you can continue to study and use linguistics after college and/or graduate school, should you wish to. We give a overview of a number of different careers in which you can apply the skills and knowledge you acquire from studying linguistics, and how you can continue to learn more about language beyond the classroom.

Interspersed throughout the book you will find boxed quotes from actual undergraduate students about what they think studying linguistics has helped them with or why they are glad they have studied linguistics. Enjoy!

2
Questions linguists ask

What is linguistics?

Linguistics is the scientific study of language. Linguists study language just like other scientists study other natural phenomena, such as photosynthesis, the solar system, DNA, or climate change. Though language has been an object of study since ancient times, from ancient Egypt, Greece, and Rome to India, China, and beyond, language scholars have had somewhat different aims, exploring different questions. Linguistics as we know it today is a relatively new field of study, based on the ideas of American linguist Noam Chomsky's 1955 *The Logical Structure of Linguistic Theory*, and subsequent works (see especially Chomsky, 1957 and 1965). The goal of what has come to be called **generative linguistics** is to understand the nature of human knowledge of language; that is, to understand that grammar is a system of rules that 'generates' all and only the grammatical sentences in a language. Linguists seek to discover what we, as speakers/signers, must know in order to produce and understand a language.

Note: When we talk about language here and throughout the book we mean both spoken and signed languages, and when we refer to a 'speaker' of a language generally, we mean any user of a spoken or signed language. We also discuss aspects of sign language specifically in several sections.

There are many ways to pursue the scientific study of language, and as in any scientific discipline, researchers have different goals, different questions to pose, and different directions of research. Some linguists study the grammar, or rule system, of a language, and others are more interested in the social factors, such as gender, age, ethnicity, and other variables, that influence how we use language. Still others study how languages change over time, how children acquire language, or how our brains process and produce language. These are just a few of the diverse ways that we can study language scientifically, and we will explore them in more detail as we progress through this book.

> "Studying linguistics has helped me to be more aware of all the amazing, intricate, and subconscious systems that allow communication to happen."

We start with the basic but important question at the heart of linguistics: *What is language?*

What is language?

A typical answer to the question *What is language?* is that language is a mode of communication. This is true, of course, but species other than humans certainly communicate as well. So do bees have language? Do whales and dolphins, wolves and chimpanzees? By exploring how some animal communication systems are similar to and different from human language, we gain some insights into the nature of human language.

Human language versus other animal communication systems

When discussing different species' communication systems it is important to first clarify the question we are asking. Here are two questions that approach the issue of animal versus human communication from different perspectives.

How are animal communication systems similar to or different from the human communication system (language)?

Can animals understand/learn/produce human language?

It is one thing to examine ways in which communication systems are similar and different (the first question), and quite another to investigate whether one species can be taught to produce and understand the communication system of another species (the second question). There are many examples of researchers who have tried to teach human language to animals (in particular to primates such as Nim Chimpsky, Washoe, Kanzi, and Koko the gorilla, with different levels of success, as in Terrace, 1979, Fouts, Fouts, & Schoenfeld, 1984, Savage-Rumbaugh & Lewin, 1994, Patterson 1978, 1981). In no known case, however, has a primate fully mastered language in the way that a human child does by age 4–5. (See, for example, Brown, 1973; Crain & Lillo-Martin, 1999.) We will explore the first question, as it provides insights into the features of human language, and helps us understand the larger question, *what is language?*

The linguist Charles Hockett came up with a list of *design features* (or characteristics) of communication systems that we can use as a starting point (Hockett, 1960). He argued that while all communication systems have some of these features, only human language has all of them. (Hockett proposed 16 features in all; we provide only a representative sample here).

Hockett's design features of language

Semanticity: signals in the system have meanings

Words have meanings in human language, and so do some of the sounds that animals make. Vervet monkeys have different calls to alert each other to different predators (leopards, eagles, and snakes: see Seyfarth, Cheney, & Marler, 1980). Prairie dogs have different barks for different predators (coyotes, skunks, and badgers: see Slobodchikoff, 1998).

> Arbitrariness: there is no logical connection between the form of the signal and what it means

There is an arbitrary connection between the word *dog* in English and the animal it refers to. We know this because the word for *dog* is different in other languages (*sobaka* in Russian; *aso* in Tagalog; *sqʷəbayʔ* in Lushootseed; *mwba* in Swahili). Animal systems also have arbitrariness: there is no logical connection between the vervet monkey's call and a snake, nor between a prairie dog's bark and a badger.

> Discreteness: messages in the system are made up of smaller parts that can be combined, rather than of single, indivisible units

Words are made up of smaller parts. For example, in human language we combine words and parts of words into larger words: *dog* + *s* = *dogs*; *dis* + *crete* + *ness* = *discreteness*. We combine single sounds into larger units: *s* + *t* + *o* + *l* combine to form the word *stole*, which we can transcribe (using the International Phonetic Alphabet) as /stol/. Sentences in turn are made up of combinations of words: *The dog stole the bone.* Vervet calls and prairie dog barks, on the other hand, can't be further broken down into meaningful parts; these sounds also cannot be combined with other sounds to express different meanings.

> Productivity: users can produce and understand messages never heard before

You have likely neither heard nor produced the sentence *There is a beautiful unicorn on my yacht*, but you understand it. There do not seem to be any animal communication systems in which signals can be recombined in ways that produce novel messages.

> Displacement: users can communicate about things that are not present

We can talk about things in the past or future, things that we hope will happen and things that happened long before we were born. Animal systems seem restricted to communicating about things in the present; Vervets don't communicate about snakes they may encounter tomorrow, and prairie dogs don't communicate about a badger they ran into last week.

It appears, then, that although animal communication systems are fascinating, and certainly worthy of study, these systems differ from human language in important ways.

Although we might be able to broadly characterize human language in terms of a series of design features, this is not the whole story, and not a complete description of our linguistic behavior. There are many other aspects of language to investigate and explore.

> "Studying linguistics has helped me to understand humans better."

What is a language?

We have briefly explored the very broad question *What is language?* We have seen that we can make some important distinctions between human language and other communication systems. But we also talk about *languages* as specific entities; we all know someone who speaks a language other than our own, and many of us have studied a language other than our own in school. The question that arises in this context is: *What is a language?*

Language variation: languages and dialects

We all know that although different speech communities may speak a single language, the actual varieties of that language spoken in each community—and even among individuals within that community—might be quite different. This makes it difficult to draw the line between what we call **a language** and **a dialect**, or variety, of that language. For example, although we might say that people in France speak French, they of course do not all speak the same variety, or dialect, of French. French varies across France and even within communities in the same region. French is also spoken in many other countries in Europe and around the world (in Belgium, Switzerland, Canada, Mauritania, Morocco, Haiti, and others). What, then, do all of these language varieties have in common and how are they different from each other, and why do we (do we?) consider them all to be varieties of the same language, *French*?

Linguists generally consider different language varieties to be dialects of the same language if the speakers of those different varieties can understand each other, if there is—as linguists call it—**mutual intelligibility**. Languages, on the other hand, are varieties that are not mutually intelligible. But this way of distinguishing languages from dialects is not always useful. Speakers of what might be called two different languages might actually be able to understand each other, but the two are nevertheless called distinct languages for political, social, or geographic reasons. This is the case for speakers of Dutch and Flemish, Swedish and Norwegian, Macedonian and Bulgarian, Malaysian and Indonesian—each is considered a different language because it is spoken in a different country, and is an important part of a speech community's identity. Serbs and Croats can understand each other perfectly well but consider their languages distinct and even use different writing systems. (The Eastern Orthodox Serbs use the Cyrillic alphabet, while the Roman Catholic Croats use the Latin alphabet.) Other speech communities may be united by a shared writing system. In China, more than a billion people speak at least seven mutually unintelligible varieties of Chinese; thus, the varieties could be considered different languages. Speakers of Cantonese, for example, cannot understand speakers of Mandarin unless they learn it as a separate language, and vice versa. However, because the people are in a single nation and because they use a single writing system, most speakers consider the various varieties to be Chinese.

Language variation therefore raises a number of interesting questions, and is the focus of much study in linguistics. For example, linguists might study how and why a language may vary over space—from region to region. Linguists have determined, for instance, that some of the **regional** differences among dialects of American English can be attributed to the different colonial settlement patterns up and down the east coast of the United States The slave trade and the contact between English and African languages also contributed to the rise of different **ethnic** varieties of English, including Gullah, spoken in the coastal areas of South Carolina, Georgia, and Florida, and African American English, spoken all over the United States. Many other variables can influence language variation, including **gender** and **sexuality**, **age, socioeconomic status**, and others. In fact, it is difficult if not impossible to study language variation in terms of a single variable or factor. We may make broad generalizations about pronunciations and vocabulary that distinguish different regional or ethnic varieties of American English, for example, but when we examine speech communities more locally, what are referred to as **communities of practice**, the linguistic landscape becomes quite a bit more complex. (See Eckert & McConnell-Ginet, 1992.)

For example, African American English (AAE), an ethnic dialect, is spoken all over the United States, and has a range of features and rules that distinguish it from other varieties of English. In AAE 'habitual' *be* indicates an ongoing state of affairs: *The coffee be cold* means *The coffee is always cold. The coffee cold*, where *be* is deleted, however, is equivalent to *The coffee is cold right now* in other varieties of American English. But AAE also varies from region to region; in Los Angeles, for example, AAE is influenced by Chicanx English (and vice versa), but the AAE spoken in Chicago is not (Wolfram & Schilling, 2015).

AAE also varies in terms of local communities of practice. Mallinson and Childs (2007) studied eight AAE-speaking women in a rural Appalachian community whose linguistic practices divided them into two groups, the 'church ladies,' who avoided certain AAE features, and the 'porch sitters,' who did not. These linguistic differences aligned with each group's different ideologies about religion, education, and femininity. The church ladies gather at church to discuss family, the Bible, and church business. Their speech is more aligned with notions of what is considered proper English and proper decorum outside of the community. The porch sitters talk about men and their neighborhood, and identify more closely with race and the activities of the local community. The language of these eight women therefore cannot be described strictly in terms of norms of ethnicity or region, but rather in terms of the complex interplay of variables that characterize their different speech communities.

The study of language variation, or **sociolinguistics**, focuses on language variation in any kind of social context. Research in sociolinguistics includes a wide range of topics and variables, and we have only provided a few examples here. But this short discussion provides us with some insights into the question *What is a language*, by illustrating how the labels we use for different languages and language varieties can obscure the dynamic and complex nature of actual linguistic practice. We discuss aspects of sociolinguistic research in more depth in Chapter 8.

> "Studying linguistics encourages welcoming and understanding of all other language varieties and their accompanying cultures without criticism of any kind, but rather analysis."

Language change

It is also hard to pin down exactly what a language is because not only do languages vary from speech community to speech community, they also change over time. Taking English as an example, we might refer to the varieties of English spoken around the world today as varieties of Present Day English (PDE), even though they vary from each other in many ways. We also assume that the language

Table 2.1 Time periods of the English language

Old English	500–1050
Middle English	1050–1450
Early Modern English	1450–1700
Present Day English	1700–present

varieties from which PDE developed over time are all also English, even though they bear little resemblance to the English of today.

Old English, *Middle English*, *Early Modern English*, and *Present Day English* refer to English spoken in the British Isles during particular historical periods. These labels and dates are arbitrary; Old English didn't change into Middle English overnight in 1050, and Middle English didn't magically morph into Early Modern English in 1450. Rather, English changed gradually over time, for a variety of reasons (social, political, cultural, and linguistic). Nevertheless, we can still study these earlier varieties of English and determine that English—at least the varieties we have records of—during these historical periods shared certain grammatical characteristics, and that these characteristics gradually changed, often as a result of historical events.

The following selection from *Beowulf* (which appeared in written form around 1000 CE) illustrates how different Old English (also referred to as Anglo-Saxon) is from Present Day English.

```
hwæt    we gardena                    in geardagum
Listen!  we of the Spear-Danes        in days-of-yore

Þeodcyninga         þrym        gefrunon
of those clan-kings the glory   have heard

hu    ða    æþelingas  ellen              fremedon
how   those nobles     courageous deeds   performed
```

'Listen! We have heard of the courageous deeds of the Danes (and) their kings in earlier times, how the noble ones accomplished courageous deeds.'

One is hard-pressed to find more than a few recognizable words in the *Beowulf* passage (*we*, *in*), and if you were to hear this passage read aloud (or sung, as it typically was at the time), you might notice that <hw> in *hwæt* is pronounced as <wh>, that <g> in *geardagum* is pronounced as <y>. You might also notice that *Þeodcyninga* is a single word rather than, as in PDE, a phrase with separate words 'of those clan-kings.'

Now jump ahead several hundred years to Chaucer's time; here we can see how the language has changed, due in part to the effects of the Viking Invasions of the British Isles from the eighth to eleventh centuries, and of the influence of Norman French, spoken by the aristocracy after the Norman Invasion of England in 1066. The following passage is from the *Prologue* to *The Canterbury Tales*, written at the end of the fourteenth century, during the Middle English period.

> A knyght ther was, and that a worthy man,
> That fro the tyme that he first bigan
> To riden out, he loved chivalrie,
> Trouthe and honour, fredom and curteisie.
> Ful worthy was he in his lordes were,
> And therto hadde he riden, no man ferre,
> As wel in cristendom as in hethenesse,
> And evere honoured for his worthynesse.

Though the word order is still different in some ways from PDE, as is some of the vocabulary and spelling, the passage is far more understandable to contemporary English speakers than the excerpt of *Beowulf*. If you were to hear this passage read aloud in Middle English, you would notice that the vowel sounds are quite different from today's, though again, you would still be able to understand quite a bit of what is being said. Some words are even identical to their PDE counterparts: *and*, *as*, *for*, *in*, *no*, *were*, and *worthy*, *tyme*, *loved*, *honour*, etc.

Consider too how word meanings have changed over time. In Middle English, a *knave* was simply a male child, not a rascal.

Nice meant 'foolish' and *silly* meant 'weak.' Around 1600 *decimate* meant 'to kill one in every ten,' and 600 years ago *myriad* meant a specific number (10,000 to be exact), rather than meaning 'a lot,' as we use it today. These words are all still in the English language, which suggests that at some point, some speech community adopted the new meaning. So we can study how a language has changed over time, what we call studying language **diachronically**, or we can study a language as it exists at a certain point in time, **synchronically**.

The study of language change includes the study of language attitudes about change. There have been attempts to create language academies to protect languages from changing; *l'Académie Francaise* was formed in 1635, and the Italian *Accademia della Crusca* in 1582, but these efforts rarely succeed. Proposals for an English Academy arose around this time as well, championed by authors including Daniel Defoe and Jonathan Swift, but the attempt ultimately failed. Though Samuel Johnson's dictionary in 1755 was recognized as a kind of authoritative work on the English language, Johnson himself later recognized and embraced the inevitability of language change. Today, dictionaries, from the venerable *Oxford English Dictionary* to the *Dictionary of American Regional English*, to the online *Urban Dictionary*, reflect how word meanings shift and change over time. Modern lexicographers are language historians, cataloging what we say and how we use language.

There are many different topics that linguists study when they study language change, or **historical linguistics**. They may trace the origins of language families, to determine how languages are related to each other. They might study the origins of the words in a language, or etymology. Still other topics include how languages change in terms of syntax or word order, or how pronunciations change over time. What precipitates change? In addition to historical events such as wars, exploration, and colonization, disease, climate, population, famine, migration, and other factors shape language change.

A *language*, then, is not a static thing that we can pin down and define; rather, languages are dynamic systems that change over time and vary over space. What we call a 'language' is actually a continuum of language varieties that have changed over time. In Chapter 7, we'll explore more of the ways in which linguists study **historical linguistics** or **diachronic linguistics**. We leave the question of *What is a language?* and turn to a related question of great interest to linguists, namely, *What does it mean to know a language?*

What does it mean to know a language?

As we mentioned in the Introduction to this book, one of the central questions linguists ask is *What does it mean to know a language?* That is, what is it that we humans need to know in order to produce and understand whatever language we speak or sign?

Our linguistic intuitions

Any English speaker, no matter where they are from, knows that the following sentence is not a natural sentence of English. (We use the linguists' convention of * to mark words or phrases that do not naturally occur in a particular language.)

*The dog at girl the barked.

Though a native English speaker can probably figure out what the sentence means based on the words in the sentence and on what they know about the world (about people and dogs), they also know that there is something odd about the order of words in this sentence, and that a more natural order would be:

The dog barked at the girl.

This suggests that native English speakers have some knowledge of **syntax**, or word order, knowledge that allows speakers to distinguish between a syntactically possible (natural) sentence of English and a syntactically impossible (unnatural) one.

There are many other ways to illustrate our intuitive knowledge of language. English speakers know, for example, that even though the sentences below look completely parallel in terms of word order, their interpretations are quite different.

The teacher is easy to please.
The teacher is eager to please.

In the *easy* sentence, the teacher is easy for someone else to please. In the *eager* sentence it is the other way around; the teacher is eager to please someone else. These differences in meaning are illustrated below.

The teacher is easy (for someone else) to please (the teacher).
The teacher is eager (for the teacher) to please (someone else).

As illustrated above, each of these sentences includes elements that we understand to be there, even though those elements are not pronounced. If there were no such understood elements, we would not be able to explain the very different interpretations of each sentence. This suggests that part of our unconscious knowledge of syntax includes knowledge of the possible word orders in our language, and of **understood elements**—structure that is there, but just not pronounced or signed—in a sentence.

There are many other such syntactic patterns and puzzles, in English and in all languages, signed or spoken, and exploring them leads us to a deeper understanding not only of our own knowledge of language, but of the structure of other languages, and how languages are similar and how they are different.

For example, consider this sentence:

The fox chased the rabbit.

Any English speaker knows that we can rearrange the order of words in this sentence in the following way:

The rabbit was chased by the fox.

We have, in this case, taken an *active* sentence and made it *passive*, something English speakers intuitively know how to do, even though it might be hard to explain exactly how it's done. English speakers also know how to form a question out of the first sentence:

Did the fox chase the rabbit?

And out of the second:

Was the rabbit chased by the fox?

Discovering the knowledge underlying word order and how pieces of sentences can be rearranged, what linguists refer to as **movement**, is a topic of much study in syntax.

Speakers also know how to interpret this sentence:

The rabbit was chased by the fox but the squirrel wasn't.

This sentence again involves *understood elements*, in this case, some syntactic material that we might think of as missing, a process that linguists refer to as **ellipsis** or **deletion**. We can represent deletion as follows:

The rabbit was chased by the fox but the squirrel wasn't ____.
The rabbit was chased by the fox but the squirrel wasn't (*chased by the fox*).

English speakers have no trouble understanding the meaning of the missing material here.

As you can see from this short discussion, speakers' knowledge of syntax includes far more than knowledge of basic word order. We also know how to interpret material that may go unpronounced; we know how to rearrange words into different possible orders; and we understand sentence structure even when material is missing or deleted.

These and other aspects of our linguistic knowledge are not the kinds of things about language that we learn from our teachers or parents or friends; this is **unconscious** knowledge of language that we are never taught. Nevertheless, language users must have this knowledge in order to produce and understand their language(s), and no native speaker knows a language better than another.

> "Studying linguistics has helped me to listen really well and pay attention when people speak. It's truly amazing how much we know without knowing we know it."

Linguistic competence and linguistic performance

Let's explore this notion of our linguistic knowledge in a little more depth. Suppose a native speaker of English makes a slip of the tongue, saying *You hissed my mystery lecture* rather than *You missed my history lecture.* Suppose someone says *hot* when they mean to say *cold*, or someone can't seem to find the right word, even though they know what they want to say. Do these things mean the speaker doesn't really *know* English, and that someone else, who doesn't make such 'errors,' knows English better? From the point of view of the linguist, not really; speech 'errors' such as slips of the tongue, errors you make when you are tired or nervous, starts and stops, and so on, are part of our **linguistic performance**. While speakers and signers may differ in terms of linguistic performance, we do not differ in terms of **linguistic competence**, our intuitive knowledge of the rule system of our native language.

Although we tend to value certain kinds of linguistic performance (Dr. Martin Luther King Jr., for example, is well known in the United States as an accomplished orator), and we may label someone as more "well spoken" than another person, these are judgments based on social criteria (incidental criteria that vary across individuals and cultures), rather than on language users' unconscious knowledge of language. The idea that there is a distinction between our unconscious knowledge of language and the language we actually produce goes back a long way (at least from the French philosopher René Descartes to Swiss linguist Ferdinand de Saussure and beyond), and this important distinction has radically changed the questions we ask about language and how we study it.

Let's take a closer look at our intuitive knowledge of language (our linguistic competence). So far, we have discussed some of the things we know about **syntax**, or word order. But there are other things we need to know about language in order to produce and understand it, including rules of pronunciation (**phonetics** and **phonology**), word structure (**morphology**), and meaning (**semantics**). These different components make up what linguists call the **grammar** of a language.

What is grammar?

Here, we briefly explore this notion of grammar, with examples from English (though we could use any language, signed or spoken, to illustrate). As you'll see, *grammar* as linguists study it is quite different from the way you may have studied grammar in school or heard about it in wider public discourse.

Our knowledge of grammar

Consider the following well-known sentence, attributed to Noam Chomsky:

Colorless green ideas sleep furiously.

Although this sentence is nonsensical, there is still something about it that seems natural; all the words are in the appropriate order for a typical English sentence. Rules of meaning, or **semantics**, are broken here, but not rules of syntax, or word order. More specifically, native English speakers know that *ideas* is an abstract, inanimate noun, and therefore can't sleep, nor can abstract nouns have colors, and be green. *Colorless* and *green* present a contradiction; something both with and without color at the same time. And *ideas*, as inanimate abstractions without volition, can't do anything *furiously.*

There are many other semantic puzzles that offer insights into this component of our linguistic knowledge. We know, for example, that the following newspaper headline is ambiguous; it has more than one meaning. What are these meanings?

Milk Drinkers Are Turning to Powder

This headline exemplifies **lexical ambiguity:** the ambiguity can be attributed to ambiguous words. The phrase *turning to* can be interpreted as 'choosing' (powdered milk over liquid) or as 'becoming' (the drinkers themselves are turning into powder). The word *powder* can also be ambiguous, meaning powdered milk or powder of some other kind.

And what about the sentence below? Assume that this one is not lexically ambiguous. What other reason could there be for its ambiguity?

They love English cotton clothes.

This sentence is **syntactically ambiguous**; its different meanings are based on syntax, not on the ambiguity of a particular word. We can explain the ambiguity by dividing the words up into groups, or phrases, in two different ways.

They love [English [cotton clothes]].
They love [[English cotton] clothes].

In the first sentence, *English* modifies *cotton clothes* (the cotton clothes are English), but in the second, *English cotton* modifies *clothes* (the clothes are made of English cotton). This sentence has two different meanings because it has two different structures!

Here's a fun one: *I love ambiguity more than most people.* Can you explain why this is ambiguous?

The study of semantics sometimes overlaps with the study of logic; we know, for example, that if a tulip is a flower and that flowers are plants, then a tulip is a plant (a logical syllogism that involves the semantic relationship of **entailment**):

A tulip is a flower
Flowers are plants
A tulip is a plant

We also understand complex relationships among words that express quantity, or what linguists call *quantifiers*. Consider the following sentence for example:

Everybody loves somebody.

This sentence has two interpretations—that everybody loves the same person (*Evan*, *Lee*, and *Cary* all love *Isabelle*) or it can mean that each person loves a different person (*Evan* loves *Lee*, and *Cary* loves *Isabelle*, and so on). These interpretations have their source in something called **quantifier scope**, the interaction between the two quantifiers *every* and *some*.

Even though we may not be familiar with the terms *ambiguity*, *entailment*, and *quantifier scope*, we, as language users, understand these and many other complex semantic relationships.

We also know quite a bit about the structure of the words in our nonsense sentence. We know, for example, that *-less*, the suffix on *color*, turns the noun *color* into an adjective, *colorless*. We also know that *-less* can be attached to other nouns like *fear*, *penny*, and *defense* (*fearless*, *penniless*, *defenseless*), but not to verbs, like *meet*, *teach*, or *resemble* (*meetless, *teachless, *resembleless). We know that *-s* on *ideas* indicates plurality, and that the *-ly* on *furiously* makes the adjective *furious* an adverb. We therefore have extensive knowledge of **morphemes**, or parts of words, and of **affixation**, the rules of suffixation and prefixation in a language like English. Even though you may not be able to describe these relationships in technical terms, part of your knowledge of English includes the knowledge of word structure, or **morphology**.

Some other examples of our morphological knowledge include knowledge of how to form new words using **word formation rules**, as illustrated below with examples of various types:

Acronyms: FOMO, SARS
Initialisms: NBA, PTA
Clipping: totes (from *totally*), pants (from *pantaloons*)
Blends: ginormous (*gigantic* + *enormous*), apathetic (*apathy* + *pathetic*)
Coining: bling, google

Compounding: bailout, upgrade
Eponyms: Achilles' heel, cardigan
Conversion: troll (as a noun and as a verb), text (from noun to verb)
Backformation: liaise (from *liaison*), enthuse (from *enthusiasm*)

A type of misinterpretation, which nevertheless illustrates how we analyze word structure, is called an **eggcorn** (a mispronunciation of *acorn*, depending on your dialect). Some eggcorns that you may be familiar with include *doggy-dog world*, for *dog-eat-dog world*, *death nail* for *death knell*, and *all intensive purposes*, for *all intents and purposes*. (Linguists have created an eggcorn database to keep track of these misinterpretations, many of which make more sense than the original pronunciations! Take a look! https://eggcorns.lascribe.net/page/1/)

In addition to rules of syntax, semantics, and morphology, we also know how to pronounce words in our language. Speakers of a language know the inventory of sounds in their language, and how those sounds can be combined. The study of the inventory of sounds is called **phonetics**, and the study of the sound system, how we combine sounds in a language, is called **phonology**.

Languages may differ in terms of their phonetic inventories, but each chooses from a set of *possible* linguistic sounds produced by the human articulatory system, which are distinct from other sounds we can make that are not linguistically meaningful (*vroom vroom, tsk, tsk*, a kissing sound, a raspberry, etc.). The International Phonetic Alphabet, or IPA, has been developed as a way of graphically representing the sounds of human language.

A phonetic transcription of an English pronunciation of the sentence we gave above, *Colorless green ideas sleep furiously*, using the symbols for English, follows:

[kʌlɹ̩lɛs gɹin ajdiəz slip fjɹ̩iəsli]

(The brackets indicate that this is written using phonetic transcription. In Chapter 3, we discuss the use of brackets [ ] compared to slashes //.)

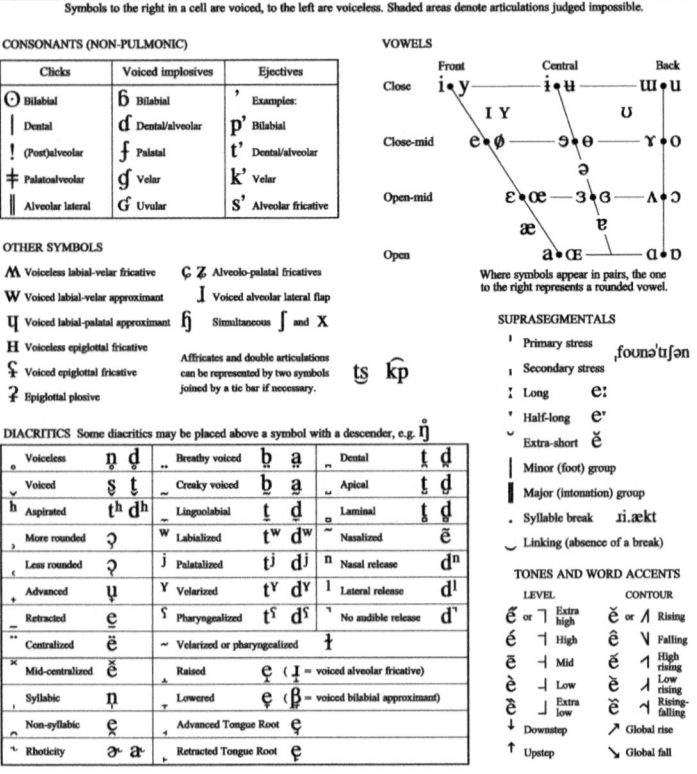

Figure 2.1 The International Phonetic Alphabet (revised to 2015)

Consider some of the ways in which linguistic inventories vary. The /r/ sound is pronounced differently in English, French, and Spanish. Arabic and Hebrew, but not English, have pharyngeal consonants. The Bantu languages Xhosa and Zulu have click consonants as part of their phonetic inventory. Samoan has neither /t/ nor /n/, sounds that occur in many other languages. Languages also have different vowel inventories; French, Portuguese, and Polish have nasal vowels, and in the Mon language of Myanmar and Thailand, vowels with high tones (tones are another phonetic distinction among languages) are pronounced with creaky or breathy voice, a pronunciation that does not exist in English in the same way.

Phonology, as we noted above, is the study of the way sounds from a language's phonetic inventory are combined. English speakers know, for example, that the plural -*s* at the end of *ideas* is actually pronounced more like the sound /z/ than the sound /s/, but that the -*s* at the end of *colorless* is pronounced /s/ rather than /z/. Speakers also know that *sleep* and *green* both begin with consonant clusters (/sl/ and /gɹ/) that we find in other English words (*slow, slovenly* and *grab, grovel*) but that we don't find words in English that start with /ls/ or /ɹg/. In fact, the longest possible sequence of initial consonants (or consonant cluster) in English is /stɹ/ as in *strike* and /spl/ as in *splat*, but in Georgian, a language spoken in the Caucasus mountains, words can begin with four, five, or even six consonants. Hawaiian and Hausa, on the other hand, have no consonant clusters at all!

Our phonological rule system accounts for other things about our pronunciations. For example, we might pronounce *I can bake* as *I cam bake* (because of a process called **assimilation**), and we might pronounce *cold cuts* as *col cuts* (due to a process of **deletion**). We also insert sounds into some words (through a process called **insertion** or **epenthesis**): *athlete* and *realtor* become *athalete* and *realator*, and we switch sounds around sometimes (**metathesis**) *cinnamon* → *ciminon, animal* → *aminal.*

Phonological rules also explain patterns of **stress**. Consider the following example, where stress shifts when we increase the number of syllables:

grámmar/grammátical/grammaticálity

But that in other words, stress remains on the same syllable, no matter how many more we add:

forgíve/forgíveable/unforgíveable/unforgíveableness

Our phonetic inventory, and how sounds are combined in a particular language, account for our different **accents**, and also account for different pronunciations among speakers of the same language, who speak different varieties, or dialects, of that language (as we discussed briefly above). In most varieties of Canadian English *Mazda* is pronounced with the vowel sound in *cat*, but in most varieties of American English with the first vowel sound in *father*. In some parts of the United States, the words *cot* and *caught* are pronounced the same (as are *don* and *dawn* and *hock* and *hawk*), but in other parts of the country, these words are pronounced differently. Many dialects of English around the world drop /ɹ/ after a vowel, characterized by the sentence *Pahk the cah in Hahvahd yahd.* (Interestingly, this well-known sentence does not accurately characterize how 'r-drop' works; speakers would pronounce the /r/ in *car* here, because it is followed by a vowel in the next word, *in*—a little known component of this rule.)

Our knowledge of syntax, semantics, morphology, phonetics, and phonology makes up what linguists refer to as our knowledge of the **grammar** of a language. This definition of grammar is likely very different from other definitions you are familiar with, and it isn't surprising, then, that the way linguists study grammar is quite different from how you may have studied grammar in school.

Though we have introduced the idea that grammar (in the sense we mean here) includes rules, these are not the kinds of rules that you may be familiar with. **Grammatical rules** in the linguist's sense are more accurately defined as the natural laws and principles that govern our biological capacity to produce and understand language. We will continue to explore the notion of grammar, and of grammatical rules, in the following sections.

Prescriptive and descriptive grammar

The definition of grammar as a system of syntactic, semantic, phonological, and morphological rules is not the definition of grammar that most people learn about. Grammar in the linguist's sense is a *description* of a language user's unconscious knowledge of grammar (rules/principles of phonetics and phonology, morphology, syntax, and semantics).

> **Descriptive grammar:** the set of unconscious rules that allow us to produce and understand a language.

Descriptive grammar differs quite dramatically from what we typically learn about grammar in U.S. schools or in popular discourse about language. You may have been told, for example, to use *whom* in certain positions instead of *who*; to write *To whom did you write the letter?* rather than *Who did you write the letter to?* You may also have been told to avoid 'double negatives' such as *I don't know nothing about that*, and to say instead *I don't know anything about that*. You may have been told to say *Owen and I went to the store*, even though it may seem more natural to you to say *Me and Owen* or *Owen and me went to the store*. We are typically taught—sometimes directly and sometimes indirectly—that certain ways of speaking and writing (what we might refer to as someone's grammar) are 'correct,' and that other ways are 'incorrect' or even 'lazy' or 'sloppy,' or flat-out wrong.

The idea that we should follow certain rules in order to speak and write English correctly has a long history, beginning in seventeenth-century England, when grammarians sought to 'fix' the language in some pure form (usually the form that corresponded with their own speech and writing, which is perhaps not surprising). These grammarians sought to *prescribe* rather than *describe* rules of language, and the sets of rules they came up with are rules of **prescriptive grammar**, rules that govern what we *should* say (according to some authority).

> **Prescriptive grammar**: rules that prescribe what we should say, according to some authority.

Prescriptive rules are very different from descriptive rules; the latter seek to describe what we *actually* say (regardless of whether someone thinks what we say is correct or not). For many speakers, sentences like *Who did you talk to?* and *I don't know nothing about that*, or the use of *ain't* or of *like* are perfectly natural, suggesting that these sentences conform to those speakers' unconscious grammatical rules. Such utterances are, from a descriptive point of view, completely **grammatical**, even if from someone's prescriptive point of view these sentences might be considered incorrect or ungrammatical, and viewed as errors, because they don't match up with whatever is taken to be, by some language authority, to be acceptable, or correct. We have all been corrected for something we've said or written by teachers, grandparents, siblings, friends, or even strangers, and we have probably also corrected others for something they have said, signed, or written that we consider wrong. We all (even linguists) have our own language pet peeves! And we are also familiar with the notion of 'grammar' not only as a list of 'dos and don'ts' of spoken language, but also as writing conventions, spelling, and punctuation rules. This view of grammar is very different from descriptive grammar, which is (ideally) based on the unconscious grammatical system that underlies languages.

As we have said above, one of the central goals of linguistics is to study language scientifically, to determine the underlying system of rules that allows us to produce and understand language. To do this, linguists must gather language **data**, by observing what speakers actually say, rather than what speakers *should* say, according to some authority. It follows, then, that the scientific study of language, or more specifically grammar, is based on descriptive grammar rather than prescriptive grammar.

This is not to say that the study of prescriptive grammar isn't also interesting and valuable. Where did these prescriptions come from, and who decides what is 'correct' and 'incorrect?' What is the legacy of prescriptive grammar today? What is the role of prescriptive grammar in education? Who is a language authority and why? Has technology changed our perceptions of what is prescriptively grammatical? These are all interesting questions, and exploring them tells us a great deal about **language attitudes** and how they shape how we perceive ourselves and others.

> "Studying linguistics has allowed me to more clearly explain to others the importance of an egalitarian attitude towards language. It is astounding to realize how language snobbery contributes to discrimination, and the degree to which people make value judgments based on prescriptive grammar and dialect. I want to help people understand these perspectives by offering them persuasive evidence, which I now have the tools to do."

Note, too, that there is not always a clear distinction between prescriptive and descriptive grammar. When you study another language in school, for example, you learn many of the descriptive grammatical rules of that language, along with some prescriptive ones. For some language users, prescriptive rules align with descriptive rules (which again tells us something about both). Suppose, for instance, that in your dialect, you would say *I didn't know anyone at the party*. A speaker of another dialect of English might say *I didn't know no one at the party*.

I didn't know anyone at the party.
I didn't know no one at the party.

Although each utterance is descriptively grammatical for the speaker of that language variety, the second version (using *no* words in negative sentences: *no one, nowhere, nothing*) can be socially stigmatized outside of the communities in which it is used, while the first version (using *any* words in negative sentences: *anyone, anywhere, anything*) may be less socially stigmatized.

I didn't go anywhere yesterday.
I didn't know anything about that.

I didn't go nowhere yesterday.
I didn't know nothing about that.

And if a speaker of a dialect that employs *I didn't go nowhere* uses the more 'school appropriate' *I didn't go anywhere* in their own speech community, this can also be stigmatized; here the speaker is adopting a structure that is not part of that speech community's dialect. Because of societal language attitudes, certain dialects are valued more highly than others, and it is often the case that the dialects more highly socially valued are those that we also assume to be aligned with prescribed rules about language.

Universal Grammar

The descriptive grammar of a language that we speak or sign can be characterized as our **mental grammar**, the set of rules that make up our unconscious knowledge of language. In fact, there is evidence that humans are 'hardwired' to acquire language, which suggests that there is some aspect of language that for humans is innate. This does not mean that we are born with the knowledge of Swahili or Ewe or Japanese imprinted in our brains, but rather that we all, under normal conditions, have the capacity to acquire the language, or perhaps more accurately, the *grammar* of the language, we are exposed to. This predisposition for language can be compared to birds' predisposition to fly; no one teaches baby birds to take wing and leave the nest, but at some point they do. Being predisposed to acquire language means that we have some innate ability to tease out the grammar of French or Bengali or Wampanoag if we are exposed to it.

Because we humans all have basically the same brain, which is hardwired in the same way biologically, linguists hypothesize that the languages that we acquire will also share the same basic blueprint, or set of basic grammatical principles. That is, all languages we acquire are *natural* languages, governed by the same set of natural laws and/or principles. This set of natural laws or principles that all languages share is sometimes referred to as **Universal Grammar (UG)**.

Assuming UG, the grammars of languages around the world will have the same basic architecture, even though on the surface they may look very different. Linguists therefore study the grammatical properties of different languages to discover the principles and properties those languages have in common, and to find explanations for the apparent differences among them.

In later sections we will provide examples of this kind of cross-linguistic research and what we learn from it. Before we do that, however, we'll briefly explore some evidence for UG and the human capacity for language.

First language acquisition

One strong piece of evidence that humans are hardwired to acquire language comes from first language acquisition. Children around the world, whether hearing, deaf, or Deaf (where capitalized Deaf refers to the Deaf culture and community), regardless of family structure and culture, acquire their first language in the same basic developmental stages as long as they are exposed to it.

Stages of first language acquisition
The babbling stage (4–8 months)
The one-word stage (9–18 months)
The two-word stage (18–24 months)
The early multiword stage (24–30 months)
The later multiword stage (30 months and older)

Children also, quite amazingly, acquire language without direct instruction; no one teaches us all the possible sentences in a language, yet we know how to produce and understand complex sentences we have never been exposed to by the time we are about 5 years old. Children's 'mistakes' also tell us quite a bit about our knowledge of language. Consider this example: suppose a child hears the sentences *We painted the green chair* and *We painted the chair green*. You might think that the child would infer that the adjective *green* and the noun *chair* can occur in two different orders (*green chair* and *chair green*). We might expect then, that when the child encounters any sentence with the order adjective + noun, that this order may be switched. But this is not the case. Though a child might produce *We painted the chair green*, she will never produce **We saw the chair green.* Why don't children make this error? Because they do not learn by analogy; their acquisition is guided by linguistic rules (in this case, the varying syntactic properties of verbs; see Pinker, 1994). There are many such examples of how child language acquisition is guided not by instruction, correction, or reinforcement, but rather by innate knowledge of language. We discuss the stages of first language acquisition in more detail in Chapter 9.

Christopher the linguistic savant

The case of a man named Christopher, a linguistic savant, provides yet more fascinating evidence for the human capacity for language and UG. Neil Smith, of University College London, and Ianthi-Maria Tsimpli, of the University of Cambridge, have long studied Christopher, a linguistic genius who knows some 20 languages with varying levels of fluency (Smith & Tsimpli, 1995) Christopher has a 'perfect' ability to acquire language even as an adult, but he is in other ways severely cognitively impaired.

In one experiment, Smith and Tsimpli tried to teach Christopher an artificial language, Epun, with properties that do not exist in actual natural languages, but which is quite easy to learn. Christopher could not master this artificial language, because, Smith and Tsimpli argue, its rules did not conform to the blueprint of natural language, Universal Grammar. In another experiment they taught Christopher some Berber, a language in which speakers can drop the subject of the sentence in ways that are impossible in English. (Berber is a 'null subject' language, as are Spanish, Modern Greek, and many others. In Spanish, for example, one can say *tengo frio* 'have cold' rather than *yo tengo frio* 'I have cold/I'm cold.' The separate pronoun *yo* 'I' does not need to be pronounced.) However, the data Smith and Tsimpli provided to Christopher never included sentences with null subjects.

Nevertheless, Christopher began producing sentences with null subjects on his own. This suggests that Christopher was able to deduce the grammatical properties of Berber from the limited linguistic input provided to him, just as children deduce grammatical properties of the language without hearing every possible sentence in their language. Christopher's language ability provides compelling evidence for an innate human capacity for language and for UG.

Contact languages and language genesis

Pidgin and creole languages also offer insights into the human capacity for language and UG. A **pidgin** language develops when two or more different languages come into contact (pidgins and creoles are therefore referred to as **contact languages**), and speakers of those languages need a way to communicate with each other. Pidgins are not 'broken' languages, as they are sometimes portrayed in the media; they are simplified linguistic rule systems that share similar features regardless of the languages they emerge from.

Pidgins have sprung up all over the world, most prominently as a result of European colonialism and the slave trade of the eighteenth and nineteenth centuries. Pidgins have developed in West Africa and the Caribbean, often based on the colonial languages English, French, Portuguese, Spanish, and Dutch, in contact with African languages. Others have emerged in the Far East (Chinese Pidgin English, Yokohama Pidgin Japanese), and in the Pacific (the Micronesian pidgin, Tok Pisin, and Hawaiian Pidgin English). Many pidgins have developed into creoles, and are spoken as native languages. (Creoles will be discussed further below.) Others are no longer spoken; Chinook Jargon (or Chinuk Wawa) was once widely spoken in the U.S. Pacific Northwest, and took features and vocabulary from Chinook, Nootka, and other languages, as well as English and French later.

In the development of a pidgin, the language of the group with less power is the **substrate** language, and the language of the group with more power is the **superstrate** language. Typically, the substrate language influences the structure and meaning of the words in the pidgin, but the words themselves are borrowed from the superstrate language.

Here are some examples of how speakers create meaning with limited vocabulary characteristic of pidgin languages. Examples are from Tok Pisin, a Melanesian creole (which began as a pidgin) spoken in Papua New Guinea. The superstrate language is English, and the substrate languages include a variety of the native Austronesian languages, especially Kuanua.

- Reduplication: *sip* 'ship,' *sipsip* 'sheep'
- Extension: *stap* 'stop' means 'be located, to remain, to continue,' and also past tense
- Compounding: *maus gras* 'mustache' and *gras belong fes* 'beard'

Some of the features (there are others) that all pidgin languages appear to share include:

- a smaller consonant and vowel inventory than most other languages
- absence of inflectional affixes (such as past tense and plural affixes)
- verb tenses are expressed by words rather than by verb conjugations
- subject-verb-object (SVO) word order
- limited vocabulary (that leads to reduplication, extension, compounding)
- simplified pronoun system
- simple sentence structure (few embedded clauses)

Here again we use examples from Tok Pisin (this example was recorded by Margaret Mead, as cited in Hall, 1966, p. 149). This is an early example of the language, in its pidgin form (written using IPA symbols, not the more standardized orthography).

```
naw mi stap rabawl. mi stap lɔng   bıglajn,        mi katam kopra.  naw
Then I stay Rabaul. I  was in      workgroup,    I cut   copra.   Then

wanfɛla mastər       bılong kampani  ɛm i-kıçım mi mi kʊk  lɔng ɛm  gɛm.
a       white man  from company   he take     me I cook for   him again

mastər king. mi   stap.  naw ol      mastar    i-kık
Mister King. I    stay.  Then all    white men were playing football

i-     kıkım em.     naw   lɛg bılɔng ɛm    i-swelup
They   kick  him.    Then  leg of     him   swell up.
```

You can see here that Tok Pisin has SVO word order (*mi katam kopra* / 'I cut copra') and that sentences are quite short and simple. Prepositions (*of, from*) are expressed by the single word *bılɔng*, and pronouns are simplified (*mi* = *I*, ɛm = *he* and *him*, *i-* = *they*). Past tense is expressed by the word *stap*, 'stay' rather than by a suffix on the verb such as *-ed*. Other verbs in the passage have no tense inflection: *katam*, 'cut,' *i-kıçım*, 'kick,' *kʊk*, 'cook,' and so on. You can also see that the words in Tok Pisin are similar to those in English, the superstrate language, but some have different meanings (*bıglajn* 'big line' = 'workgroup,' *mastər* 'master' = 'white man,' etc.).

Over time, a pidgin can become more and more grammatically complex, and can eventually be acquired by children as a native language. At this point, the pidgin has developed into a **creole**, a language with a full-fledged grammatical system (Tok Pisin, Hawaiian Creole English, Jamaican Creole, Haitian Creole, Krio in Sierra Leone, among many others). Creole languages share some features with pidgins, and they also share features that are not found in non-creole languages. One of the most striking features of creole languages is the complex tense and aspect system. Below are some examples from three creole languages, Hawaiian Creole (English superstrate), Haitian Creole (French superstrate), and Sranan (English based, spoken in Suriname). (In French, *marcher* is 'to walk'.)

Table 2.2 Creole language comparisons

Hawaiian Creole English	Haitian Creole	Sranan
he walk (he walked)	il maché	a waka
he bin walk (he had walked)	il té maché	a ben waka
he stay walk (he is/was walking)	l'ap maché	a e waka

Source: (adapted from Bickerton, 1983)

There is much more to say about the features of both pidgin and creole languages, and about how these new linguistic systems emerge from language contact. What is important to note here is that pidgin and creole languages around the world share certain characteristics, regardless of the contact languages from which they emerge. One way to explain this striking similarity is to propose that in language contact situations, the human brain creates language based on certain universal principles of UG, and thus that these similarities are not accidental but rather are the result of our hardwiring for language.

How do we study language scientifically?

As we have mentioned above, there are many ways to study language scientifically. We have briefly discussed some of the topics that sociolinguists and historical linguists study, and we have also seen that language acquisition and our biological capacity for language are important areas of research. The branch of linguistics that specifically focuses on studying the grammar of a language in order to discover the rules of syntax, semantics, morphology, phonetics, and phonology that make up speakers' unconscious knowledge of language is sometimes referred to as **theoretical** or **formal linguistics**. Linguists who focus on grammatical structure attempt to construct a model, or theory, of speakers' linguistic knowledge. Research in this branch of linguistic theory typically does not address social factors or context, but rather relies more on native speaker judgments about natural language, though theoretical linguistics also uses corpus data and psycholinguistic experimentation.

> "There are so many reasons I'm glad I'm studying linguistics! Linguistics has helped me to approach language scientifically, to appreciate the beauty of language, and to be excited by the possibilities of being surrounded by ambient language data that always leaves me with interesting questions to think about."

In this section we provide only one example of how linguists study language scientifically. In later chapters, we discuss in more depth core areas of study in linguistics including phonetics and phonology, morphology and syntax, semantics and pragmatics, as well as how children acquire language, how language varies from region to region and community to community and even person to person, and how language changes over time.

Gathering and analyzing data: the scientific method

Thus far, we have discussed some of the questions linguists seek to answer, and we have asserted that linguists study language scientifically in order to find answers to these questions. We have yet to explain, however, how one actually does this. Researchers in other sciences, such as chemistry, physics, or biology, study phenomena that we can often observe and experiment with: melting polar ice caps, gravity, planetary motion, and so on. Scientists **observe** the world around them and ask **questions** about physical phenomena (Why is the sky blue? At what temperature does ice melt?) and **gather and study data** in order to formulate possible answers to these questions. Scientific inquiry therefore involves **forming** explanations, or **hypotheses**, about data, and then testing those hypotheses against additional data to see if they hold up. Scientists routinely **revise hypotheses** based on those data. Sets of hypotheses **make predictions**, and taken together, one can then **propose a theory** of how to account for a particular phenomenon.

Below is a model of scientific inquiry, or the scientific method.

> **Scientific method**
>
> make observations → ask questions → gather data → form hypotheses → make predictions → gather more data → test and revise hypotheses → make predictions → propose theory → repeat

But how do we study language in this way? Language is, after all, not a physical object. Indeed, once we utter a word or form a sign, language seems to disappear into thin air. But in fact, there are limitless questions that we can ask about language, and there is a wealth of data to explore. Below, we provide an example of how we might study (a very specific) syntactic phenomenon in English using scientific inquiry.

> "After studying linguistics, I finally understand what science really means—that it's not biology or chemistry, but it's a method of inquiry. And it's been so exciting to discover that using language data!"

An example of scientific inquiry: english wh-question formation

One topic of scientific research in linguistics is syntactic theory, where linguists attempt to construct a model of sentence structure. The goal is to not only explain syntactic phenomena in a particular language, but to try to determine what syntactic properties all languages have in common. One phenomenon that occurs across languages is *question formation*; all languages seem to have a way of formulating questions, though they might differ syntactically and in other ways. As a starting point for researching question formation, we will take a look at what we refer to as **wh-question formation** in English.

Here is an English sentence that any English speaker would consider grammatical:

Kim saw Cary with Lee.

And here is some more data—another natural English sentence:

Kim saw Cary and Lee.

These data seem pretty uninteresting. But we also might observe that we can form a question from the first sentence. In English, we do this via **movement**: we move an interrogative phrase, here, the word *who*, to sentence-initial position:

*Kim saw Cary with **Lee**.*
*Kim saw Cary with **who**.*
***Who** did Kim see Cary with___? (who = Lee)*

But notice that we can't form a question like this from the second sentence:

*Kim saw Cary and **Lee**.*
*Kim saw Cary and **who**.*
*Who did Kim see Cary and___?

Our two non-interrogative sentences look similar in terms of numbers of words and basic word order. The only difference is that in the first sentence the noun phrase *Lee* is preceded by *with*, and in the second, by *and*. So why can we form a question only from the first sentence but not the second?

We have determined that the only apparent difference between these two sentences is the words *with* and *and*. Linguists who study syntax know (based on much investigation of **syntactic categories**, or parts of speech) that these two words fall into different classes, or categories: *with* is a **preposition**, but *and* is a **conjunction**.

Prepositions: *to/at/by/to/with/for/about/after* etc.
Conjunctions: *for/and/nor/but/or/yet/so*

A linguist might **form the hypothesis**, then, that we can make questions with phrases following prepositions, but not with phrases following conjunctions, and that this has something to do with the syntactic differences between these two categories (preposition and conjunction). If this hypothesis is on the right track, it **predicts** that other prepositions will pattern like the *with* sentence and allow *wh*-question formation, but that sentences with conjunctions other than *and* will not.

Let's **gather more data** and **test our hypothesis**. We find that, as predicted, a sentence with a different preposition (*to*) allows *wh*-question formation, but one with a different conjunctions (*or*) does not.

Pete sells books to the students.   *Who does Pete sell books to ___?*
Pete sells books or magazines.   **What does Pete sell books or ___?*

By testing our hypothesis and the predictions it makes, even in this very limited way, we find further evidence that we can form *wh*-questions in sentences with phrases that follow prepositions, but not with those that follow conjunctions. These data support our hypothesis that prepositions and conjunctions, and the phrases they occur with, are syntactically different, even though in the sentences we are considering, this difference is not immediately apparent.

But now a new question emerges: what exactly is that difference? We want to *explain* why question formation works like it does, so we need to dig deeper.

As it turns out, there is a great deal of additional evidence that prepositions and conjunctions are syntactically distinct. Based on examining a wide range of additional data, linguists propose the schematic representation of this syntactic difference presented in Figure 2.2.

In the *with* sentence, the preposition forms a syntactic unit, or prepositional **phrase**, with its noun phrase (NP) object. This

```
          S
         / \
        NP  VP
        |   /\
        N  V  NP  PP
        |  |  |   /\
       Kim saw N  P  NP
              |  |   |
             Cary with N
                       |
                      Lee
```

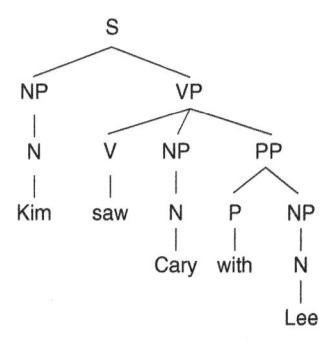

Figure 2.2

prepositional phrase is labeled PP, because the **head** of the phrase (the main word) is a preposition.

A *phrase*, then, is a syntactic unit that consists of at least a *head*, and possibly another phrase. In Figure 2.2 above, NP, VP, and PP are all phrases. (S, for 'sentence,' is also technically a phrase, but we'll leave that aside for now.)

In Figure 2.3 below for the sentence with the conjunction *and*, the NP and VP are phrases (and there is no PP).

Figure 2.3 differs from Figure 2.2 with the PP *with Lee*. In the previous tree, the preposition *with* forms a phrase with the NP, *Lee*. In this tree, however, with the conjunction *and*, the NP *Lee* is conjoined to another phrase, NP *Cary*. The larger NP *Cary and Lee* forms a phrase with the V *saw*, resulting in the VP *saw Cary and Lee*.

We might hypothesize, then, that we form *wh*-questions only of NPs that form a phrase with another word (objects of prepositions, and objects of verbs, for example). We predict that the NP object of the preposition in Figure 2.2 can be questioned:

Who did Kim see Cary with___? (*who* = Lee)

And that an NP in a conjoined NP cannot form a question.

*Who did Kim see Cary and___? (*who* = Lee)

```
          S
         / \
        NP  VP
        |   / \
        N  V   NP
        |  |   / \
       Kim saw NP and NP
              |       |
              N       N
              |       |
             Cary    Lee
```

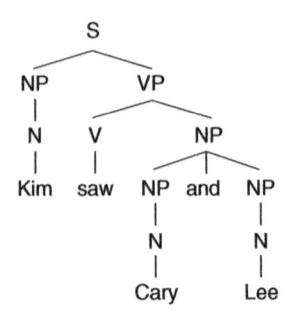

Figure 2.3

(We won't get into the details of the structure of questions here, such as what happens to the tense and why an auxiliary verb *did* is added when the statement becomes a question: Kim saw Cary with Lee → Who did Kim see Cary with?)

But note that we also predict that we should be able to form a question of the *entire* conjoined NP object of the verb *saw* in Figure 2.3—the (large) NP object [Cary and Lee]. This prediction is borne out:

Who did Kim see? *(who* = Cary and Lee)

Technical details aside, the important point here is that even though sentences may look superficially alike in terms of word order, on further investigation, we find that they can actually have very different internal structures, even though this difference is not immediately observable. And those syntactic differences provide us with a way to explain syntactic patterns, such as those we saw with *wh*-question formation in English. By studying linguistic data scientifically, we uncover the underlying structure of sentences and find explanations for phenomena that otherwise would remain mysterious.

This is just a micro-example of how a linguist might go about studying language (in this case, the syntax of *wh*-question formation) scientifically. Regardless of the technical details (the process of any kind of scientific inquiry is a process, and therefore difficult to explain without some level of detail), this brief example illustrates how it is indeed possible to gather data, form hypotheses, make predictions, and test those hypotheses against additional data. We are therefore able to, ultimately, **construct a theory** of *wh*-question formation, a series of hypotheses that predict when question formation is possible, and when it is not.

> "Studying linguistics has helped me to (1) analyze data, (2) become a better researcher, (3) appreciate diversity. I'm so happy I have come to learn more about this field."

Exploring data from other languages

Linguists who study syntactic phenomena such as *wh*-question formation in a particular language are also interested in how that phenomenon works in other languages, and/or if other languages even have *wh*-question formation at all! Exploring data from a range of other languages provides us with a bigger picture of syntactic structure and UG, and of how questions operate *across* languages. Theories we might construct from such data tell us more about the common properties that languages share around the world, and help us explain why and how they are different.

For example, we've seen that in English, the *wh*-word or phrase appears in sentence-initial position in *wh*-questions. But now let's look at how other languages form questions.

Consider French, a language that has SVO word order like English.

```
S     V      O
Tu  manges une pomme.
You  eat   an  apple
```
'You are eating an apple.'

And like English, French forms *wh*-questions of the NP object of the verb with the *wh*-word or phrase in sentence-initial position:

    O   S   V
Qu'est-ce que tu manges ___?
what is-it that you eat
'What are you eating?'

We might hypothesize from these data that SVO languages form *wh*-questions as in English and French. We might also hypothesize that this is the only way languages form *wh*-questions——the question word or phrase occurs in sentence-initial position.

But when we look at more language data, we find that neither of these hypotheses hold up.

Aleut, or Unangam Tunuu, a language spoken in the Aleutian Islands, Pribilof Islands, and the Commander Islands, has subject-object-verb (SOV) word order, unlike English and French. (The object of the verb is in boldface here.) (Data from Michael Lestenkof, personal communication.)

    S   O   V
Piitrax̂ **Ivaanax̂** ilaĝulix̂.
Peter   John   help
'Peter is helping John.'

Aleut does have *wh*-question formation, but not as in English. In Aleut, the *wh*-word or phrase occurs in the same position as it does in non-questions.

    S   O   V
Piitrax̂ **kiin** ilaĝulix?
Peter who help
'Who is Peter helping?'

This suggests that our hypothesis that all languages form *wh*-questions with the question word or phrase in sentence-initial position fails to explain the data; in some languages (such as

Unangam Tunuu) the question word stays put. We might hypothesize, then, that this is because Aleut has subject-object-verb word order (SOV) rather than SVO. So we might hypothesize that only SVO languages form questions with the question word or phrase in sentence-initial position.

But consider Chinese, which, like English, has SVO word order.

```
S     V      O
ni    maile  pingguo
you   bought apples
'You bought apples.'
```

Even though Chinese has SVO word order like English, *wh*-questions are formed as they are in Unangam Tunuu, where the question word stays put, in the same position that the object would be in non-questions.

```
S     V      O
ni    maile  shenme?
you   bought what
'What did you buy?'
```

These data make us question our hypothesis yet again. Clearly, there is no one single way to form such information-seeking questions across languages, and it's also clear that word order alone does not predict how a language will form these questions. But what we do see is that there are at least two different ways to form questions: the question word or phrase occurs sentence-initially as in English and French, or it occurs 'in-situ,' as in Unangam Tunuu and Chinese.

As you can see from this short discussion, there is much left to discover about how question formation operates across languages, and the more language data we study, the more we gain insights into this phenomenon. As in other areas of scientific inquiry, there is always more data to study that leads us to revise our hypotheses. Studying language scientifically, just like studying other biological phenomena, is an ongoing process of discovery.

In this chapter we have explored some of the basic questions about language that linguists strive to answer, and we provided a brief overview of how linguists study language scientifically to construct theories of language that attempt to answer those questions.

In the course of exploring these questions, in order to provide you with a better idea of what linguistics is, we touched on some of the main areas of study in linguistics:

- the study of grammar (phonetics and phonology, morphology, syntax, semantics)
- the study of how languages change over time
- the study of how language varies by community, location, situation
- the study of how language is acquired, produced, and processed in the brain

In the next few chapters, we delve into each of these areas of study in more depth, to provide an overview of some of the diverse and overlapping kinds of research that linguists do. We have already introduced the notion of *grammar* as the system of rules of phonetics and phonology, morphology, syntax, and semantics, our unconscious knowledge of language. Suppose you wanted to study one or more of these areas in depth? What kinds of things would you study, and what kinds of questions would you, a language scientist, ask? We will return to each area of the study of grammar mentioned here to further explore how and why linguists study it.

References

Bickerton, D. (1983). Creole languages. *Scientific American, 249*(1), 116–122.

Brown, R. (1973). *A first language: The early stages*. Cambridge, MA: Harvard University Press.

Chomsky, N. (1955). *Logical structure of linguistic theory*. Manuscript.

Chomsky, N. (1957). *Syntactic structures*. The Hague, The Netherlands: Mouton.

Chomsky, N. (1965). *Aspects of the theory of syntax*. Cambridge, MA: MIT Press.

Crain, S., & Lillo-Martin, D. (1999). *An introduction to linguistic theory and language acquisition.* Oxford, England: Blackwell.

Eckert, P., & McConnell-Ginet, S. (1992). Think practically and look locally: Language and gender as community-based practice. *Annual Review of Anthropology, 21,* 461–490.

Fouts, R., Fouts, D.H., & Schoenfeld, D. (1984). Sign language conversational interaction between chimpanzees. *Sign Language Studies, 42*(1), 1–12.

Hall, R.A. (1966). *Pidgin and creole languages.* Ithaca, NY: Cornell University Press.

Hockett, C. (1960). The origin of speech. *Scientific American, 203,* 88–96.

Mallinson, C., & Childs, B. (2007). Communities of practice in sociolinguistic description: Analyzing language and identity practices among black women in Appalachia. *Gender and Language, 1–2,* 173–206.

Patterson, F. (1978). Linguistic capabilities of a young lowland gorilla. In F.C. Peng (Ed.), *Sign language and language acquisition in man and ape: New dimensions in comparative pedolinguistics* (pp. 161–201). Boulder, CO: Westview Press.

Patterson, F. (1981). Ape language. Science, *211*(4477), 86–87. doi:10.1126/science.211.4477.86-a

Pinker, S. (1994). *The language instinct.* New York, NY: Penguin.

Savage-Rumbaugh, S., & Lewin, R. (1994). *Kanzi: The ape at the brink of the human mind.* New York, NY: John Wiley and Sons.

Seyfarth, R.M., Cheney, D.L., & Marler, P. (1980). Monkey responses to three different alarm calls: Evidence of predator classification and semantic communication. *Science, 210,* 801–803.

Slobodchikoff, C. (1998). The language of prairie dogs. In M. Tobias & K. Solisti-Mattelon (Eds.), *Kinship with the animals* (pp. 65–76). Hillsboro, OR: Beyond Words Publishing.

Smith, N., & Tsimpli, M.I. (1995). *The mind of a savant: Language learning and modularity.* Oxford, England: Blackwell.

Terrace, H. (1979). *Nim.* New York, NY: Knopf.

Wolfram, W., & Schilling, N. (2015). *American English* (3rd ed.). Malden, MA: Wiley-Blackwell.

3

The study of sound
Phonetics and phonology

We have already acquainted you with the inventory of sounds across languages, sounds that we can describe and transcribe using the **International Phonetic Alphabet**, or IPA. We briefly discussed how different languages may have different inventories of sounds, and some of the ways that sounds are produced and perceived. We discussed **stress** rules, and some of the different processes, including **assimilation, deletion, insertion/epenthesis**, and **metathesis**, that account for our pronunciations and **accents**. In this chapter, we discuss in more depth the ways that linguists study sound production and perception.

Articulatory phonetics

Phoneticians are interested in how sounds are produced and perceived. Why do sounds that are 'difficult' to pronounce—which involve many more muscles and tongue gymnastics—persist in languages? The English 'th' sounds like in *thick* or *though* are technically difficult, and children don't always acquire them right off the bat. Why then have they lasted in so many English dialects? (Some dialects of English, such as Irish English and varieties of African American English, have dispensed with these sounds; *this* and *that* are pronounced *dis* and *dat*). And the American English 'r' sound is also a sound that is 'hard' to produce and which is acquired late in child language acquisition. Phoneticians describe sounds in terms of where they are produced in the vocal tract, and in how they are produced and how the air is stopped or constrained. As we saw in Chapter 2, we can transcribe sounds of language using the International Phonetic Alphabet. Figure 3.1 is a version of the IPA that includes just the consonant sounds of (most varieties) of English.

Articulatory phonetics is the study of how we produce sounds. How, for example, does /f/ differ from /v/ or /p/ differ from /b/? These differ (only) in **voicing**, vibration of the vocal cords.

/p/ = voiceless bilabial stop
/b/ = voiced bilabial stop

Phoneticians also analyze the **place of articulation** (where in the vocal tract the sound is made); /f/ is made with the top teeth on the lower lip, a labiodental, and thus differs from /s/, made with the tongue tip on the alveolar ridge, just behind the teeth; its place of articulation is alveolar.

/f/ = voiceless labiodental fricative
/s/ = voiced alveolar fricative

Or consider the final sound of words like *ring* or *chanting*. Despite the fact that we write this with two letters, this is a single sound, which is indicated by the symbol /ŋ/, called *engma*. It's made by vibration of the vocal cords (voicing), raising the back of the tongue towards the velum, and passing air through the nose.

/ŋ/ = voiced velar nasal

See Figure 3.1 to see the descriptive terms for these various articulators and the diagram of the head in Figure 3.2 to see where in the vocal tract they are located.

Sounds are also described by the **manner of articulation** (how the airflow is obstructed, in the case of consonants, to produce a particular sound). Manner of articulation distinguishes, for example, the bilabial stop /b/ for which airflow is temporarily stopped, from the nasal /m/ for which airflow comes out the nose.

The Consonant Phonemes of English			Place of Articulation						
			bilabial	labiodental	interdental	alveolar	palatal	velar	glottal
Manner of Articulation	stop	voiceless	p			t		k	ʔ
		voiced	b			d		g	
	fricative	voiceless		f	θ	s	ʃ		h
		voiced		v	ð	z	ʒ		
	affricate	voiceless					tʃ		
		voiced					dʒ		
	nasal	voiceless							
		voiced	m			n			ŋ
	liquid	lateral voiced				l			
		rhotic voiced				ɹ			
	glide	voiceless							
		voiced	w						

Figure 3.1 Consonant phonemes of American English

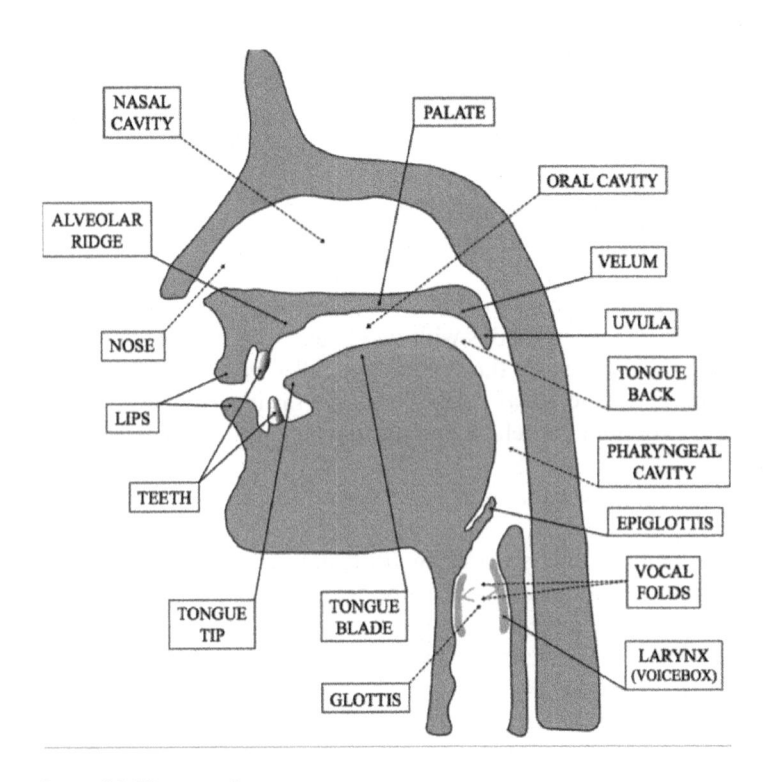

Figure 3.2 The articulators
Image courtesy of Russell Hugo

/b/ = voiced bilabial stop
/m/ = voiced bilabial nasal

These articulatory descriptions account for cross-linguistic differences as well. The /ɹ/ of English is typically bunched, while it is produced further back in German, a **uvular** 'r', which is represented by the symbol /ʀ/, and in Spanish, it is a trilled one, represented by the symbol /r/.

Vowels are also described in terms of where and how they are made—whether they are made with lip **rounding** or not; whether they are made with the tongue **high**, **mid**, or **low** in the mouth, as well as front, central, or back. The degree of muscle, of articulatory 'effort,' separates **tense** vowels from **lax** vowels. A chart such as Figure 3.3 shows the vowels of most varieties of English.

It can be useful to describe sounds in terms of their articulatory features so that we can discuss the similarities and differences of sound production across languages and dialects, language acquisition by children, second language acquisition by adults, speech delays, and language variation.

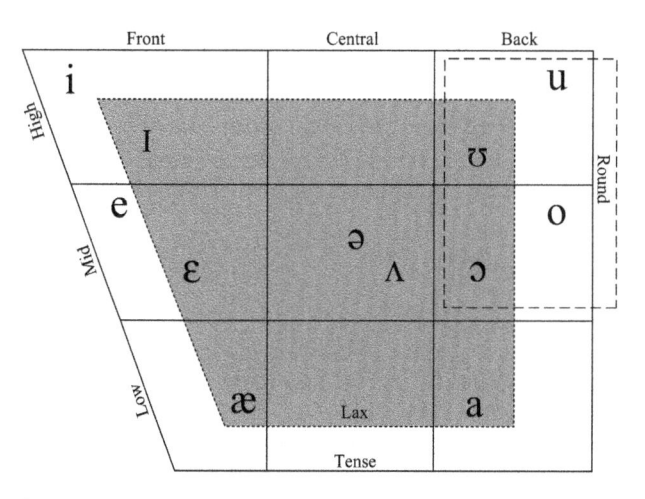

Figure 3.3 English vowels

For example, children acquiring a language may acquire some sounds later than others since some involve more articulatory effort. The English /θ/ as in the word *think* or /ð/ as in *though* may not be acquired until age 5 or 6, and the English /ɹ/ may be acquired even later, so that it's not unusual for a 9- or 10-year-old American-English-speaking child to not produce the /ɹ/ in a word like *berry*.

Or consider that it can be difficult for monolingual English speakers to produce a Spanish /r/ since the English /ɹ/ is a distinct sound. Or German-speaking adults speaking English may pronounce the word *dog* as /dak/ with a /k/ instead of /g/ since it is a rule of German phonology to 'devoice' a consonant at the end of a word. (The German word *Hund*, for example, meaning 'dog' is pronounced with a /t/ at the end.) And Japanese speakers learning English may have a difficult time discerning the English sounds /l/ and /ɹ/. In English these are distinct sounds; to English speakers, then, the sounds seem quite different from each other, even though you can see by looking at the consonant chart that the /l/ and /ɹ/ phonemes are similar in terms of their place and manner of articulation. However, Japanese, as well as Korean, Hawaiian, and other languages, does not make a distinction between /l/ and /ɹ/.

And the 'same' sound can vary in systematic ways for speakers of the same language, depending on their dialect. For example, the way *caught* is pronounced by a Wisconsite is different from the way a Virginian pronounces it. The vowels may be the same sounds on the vowel chart, but differ in patterned and interesting ways, opening up lots of possibilities for further study.

Phonological rules

Recall from Chapter 2 how a phrase like *I can bake* can sound more like *I cam bake*. An understanding of phonetics and phonological rules can explain why that is. This particular process is due to a phonological rule called **assimilation**, the process of one sound becoming more like another with respect to a phonetic feature. In this case, the alveolar /n/ becomes the bilabial /m/ to be more like the bilabial /b/ that follows, allowing for an easier transition from one sound to the next.

Assimilation is also why the final sound in the word *dogs* sounds like [z] rather than [s], as it does in *cats*. And this subconscious rule that English speakers have allows us to determine the appropriate plural sound for any noun, even ones we've never heard before or made-up words. Jean Berko Gleason conducted a now well-known experiment in 1958 with young children, demonstrating their ability to form the appropriate plurals for words they'd never heard before. "What's the plural of *wug*?" the investigators showed the children a picture of a bird-like creative, dubbed a *wug*. "This is a *wug*. Now there is another one. There are two of them. There are two ____." The children invariably replied *wugs*, pronounced with a /z/ at the end. And if we encounter another invented creature and word, say a *tark*, we know that more than one is *tarks* with /s/ as the plural. There is a principle governing these pluralizations; we don't have to learn which plural to use with which words. It turns out that /s/, a voiceless sound, follows sounds that are also voiceless, maintaining no vibration of the vocal cords, while /z/, a voiced sound, follows sounds that do have vibration of the vocal cords. Native speakers follow this rule of assimilation automatically and without instruction or conscious awareness.

There are other rules too that speakers of languages follow—sometimes making sounds more distinct from each other. This process, known as **dissimilation**, happened historically when the word *turtle* used to have two /ɹ/ s: *turtur*. But the second one changed to /l/ to make the words more dissimilar.

Sometimes sounds exchange places, known as **metathesis**. For example, *ask* can be pronounced with the /s/ and /k/ exchanging places, as was the case in Old English, and still is for many speakers. This exchange happens also with the word *asterisk*, which can be pronounced with the final two sounds switched: *asteriks*. And *bird* used to be *brid*; *wasp* used to be *waps*. Or consider the mismatch between the spelling of *iron* and its common pronunciation, which involves switching—metasthesizing—the vowel and the /ɹ/; it's not *i-ron* but *i-orn*.

Sometimes phonological rules involve **insertion** of a sound, as when a word like *realtor* has an vowel added between the /l/ and the /t/, resulting in a pronunciation like real-a-tor. Other times, there is **deletion** of a sound. Consider a word like *fifths* /fɪfθs/ or *sixths* /sɪksθs/ in which three fricatives occur in a row. One or even two of them is typically deleted in casual speech, so the pronunciation is actually /fɪfs/ or /fɪθs/ or even /fɪs/. Or consider the compound word *tennis shoes*, which is rarely pronounced with the /s/ at the end of *tennis*—that /s/ is deleted.

Importantly, all of these phonological processes for all speakers are always patterned and systematic, never random; they are *rules* of each language or dialect.

Auditory phonetics

Acoustic phonetics is the study of the physical production of sounds, in terms of frequency, pitch, duration, and other factors, as discussed above. **Auditory phonetics** is the study of how sounds are perceived by the human ear or recognized and processed by the human brain. Linguists might investigate how such phrases like *I scream* and *ice cream* are distinct phonetically and conduct experiments to better understand how they are processed similarly and differently. (Or compare *that's tough* versus *that stuff*, *mice eat* versus *my seat*.) How and why do we "mishear" song lyrics, for example, and what sorts of factors—including context—might affect that? Is it *this guy* or *the sky*?

Auditory phonetics also includes the study of **pitch** (how high or low we perceive a sound to be), **intensity** (how loud or soft we perceive a sound to be), and **duration** (how long or short we perceive a sound to be).

The kind of investigation conducted to better understand the processing of sounds is not only connected to phonetics, but also is a part of psycholinguistics and cognitive science.

Allophones and phonemes

And consider another way in which sounds can vary across languages phonetically, the **duration** of the sound. Some speech sounds simply last longer than others. In English, a vowel preceding a voiced consonant is longer than the same vowel before a voiceless consonant. Can you hear that the vowel actually lasts longer when you say *bead* than when you say *beat*? Or that *bid* is longer than *bit*? And although there are such vowel variations in English, those variations are not **distinctive**; that is, it doesn't change the meaning of a word. So, there's not one word [bɪt], to use the phonetic transcription, and another one [bɪːt] (where ː indicates a longer duration of a sound). If you drew out the vowel in *bit*, it would just sound like a slightly strange version of the same word. But vowel length is distinctive in other languages. In Finnish, for example, the difference in the length of vowels and consonants can make a difference in the meaning of a word. There's a word pronounced [muta], which means *mud*, and if you pronounce those same sounds but simply make the first vowel last longer, it means *some other*: [muːta] (where the ː indicates an elongated vowel). The same is true in Japanese: [toːkai] means *collapse*, but with a shorter vowel, [tokai], it means *city*.

So determining how the slight variations in sound production vary across languages is an important piece of phonetic and phonological investigation. You can't simply listen to a language and know its sounds: the actual sounds produced are not the sounds that matter in any given language. To see this more clearly, hold your hand or a piece of paper in front of your mouth and say the words *pit* and *spit*. When you say *pit* you should feel a puff of air that you don't feel when you say *spit*—or at least not to the same degree. This puff of air is called **aspiration**, and the difference in the way the two [p]s are pronounced results in two phonetically distinct [p]s.

Native speakers of English, however, are not even aware of the distinctions in the way the sounds are produced because the differences don't matter in English. The [p] with the aspiration and the [p] without the aspiration always occur in different positions with a word. Aspirated [p], written as [pʰ], occurs at the beginning of a stressed syllable, while unaspirated [p] occurs everywhere else. Similarly, the /t/ of *tack* is aspirated, but the /t/ of *stack* is not; the /k/ of *kit* is aspirated, but the /k/ of *skit* is not. You can feel the aspiration on the words that start with the voiceless stops /p/, /t/, and /k/

(*pat*, *cat*, *tat*) and it's not there with words that have another sound preceding (*spat*, *scat*, *stat*). This is a phonological rule or process of English that speakers follow subconsciously. The two [p]s are **allophones** of the phoneme /p/; they are predictable pronunciations of the /p/ that occurs in the IPA consonant chart. The consonant chart does not represents all of the sounds of English, but only the **phonemes** of English. The [pʰ], for example, although it is phonetically distinct from [p], is not a phoneme. Note that, by convention, the allophones are written using square brackets, while the phonemes are written inside slashes.

```
     /p/ = phoneme
     /  \
   [p]  [pʰ] = allophone
```

Although aspirated and unaspirated sounds don't make a difference in meaning in English, in certain other languages, aspiration does make a difference to speakers and can result in distinct phonemes. For example, to speakers of Hindi and Korean, these two distinct [p]s can make a difference in the meaning of a word. In Korean, /pʰal/ with an aspirated [p] means 'arm,' while /pal/ means 'foot.' The same aspiration contrast exists for the other voiceless stops, /t/ and /k/.

| /tʰal/ | 'mask' | /kʰal/ | 'knife' |
| /tal/ | 'moon | /kal/ | 'will go' |

Phonemes, therefore, are the subconscious representations of the phonological units of a language. They demonstrate the contrast between what we think we say and what we actually say. Though we aren't consciously aware of the phonemes of our language, we are perfectly aware subconsciously and are able to follow the rules of the phonology of our language effortlessly.

Syllables

It is actually difficult to provide a neat definition of a **syllable**, though we are really good at intuitively knowing what they are, and we all have awareness of syllables naturally and subconsciously. Very young children are able to tap out syllables; many phonological processes refer to syllables of words; and children (and adults) manipulate syllables quite skillfully in all sorts of ways. We manipulate syllables in poetry intentionally, and the writing of poems includes haiku, sonnets, odes—all those poems that make use of various pentameters (iambic, trochaic, dactylic, anapestic, which refer to the number of syllables in a line). Many of the writing systems of the world's languages use symbols to represent syllables (not individual sounds), called syllabaries (not alphabets). Sequoyah is well known for creating a writing system for Cherokee based on syllables.

Languages have varying syllable structures that speakers have subconscious knowledge of. The group of consonants at the beginning of a syllable is called the **onset**, and the vowel and any consonants following it at the end of the syllable are called the **rime** (also sometimes spelled *rhyme*). Linguists represent the structure of syllables in this way:

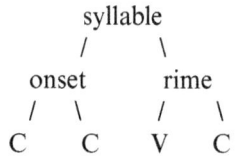

```
       syllable
       /     \
    onset    rime
    / \      / \
   C   C    V   C
```

The rime can be further divided into a **nucleus**, a vowel that is the rime, and a coda, the consonant(s) at the end of the rime.

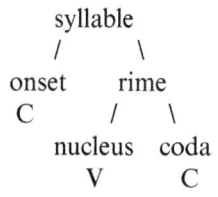

```
       syllable
       /     \
    onset    rime
     C       / \
        nucleus coda
           V     C
```

Vowels are almost always the nucleus of a syllable. However, if the syllable lacks a vowel, certain consonants are able to take over as the nucleus of the syllable. Consider the the sound at the end of the word *runner* when said in casual speech. There's not much of a vowel there, for most speakers; that vowel—which is a necessary component of a syllable—can sometimes be subsumed into those very 'sonorant' consonants when the syllables are unstressed. (More on stress below.)

Phonological processes demonstrate a subconscious awareness of syllable structure; for example, consider that some sounds are possible only in certain positions in a syllable. The sound /ŋ/ is quite common in English syllables as the coda, as in *sing*, transcribed phonetically as /siŋ/, but cannot occur as the onset of a syllable in English. In fact, it even seems really difficult to pronounce, even though English speakers have no problem pronouncing it at the end of a syllable. Try saying /ŋis/—our subconscious rules about syllable structure prevent certain sounds and certain combinations of sounds in certain positions within the syllable.

Consider too that some sounds can only occur next to each other if they are in separate syllables. For example, the /kn/ combination disappeared long ago in English pronunciation, so words like *knight* and *knee* are pronounced without the /k/ that used to be there, and it seems hard to even say. But across syllables, we can produce the /k/-/n/ next to each other without a problem, as in *acne*.

Other sounds are pronounced differently depending on where they occur within a syllable. There are two distinct /l/ sounds for most English speakers, known as clear [l] and dark [ɫ]. Compare the way /l/ is pronounced in the following word pairs; /l/ at the end of the syllable is [ɫ], while /l/ at the beginning is [l], for most speakers (the - indicates the break between syllables):

bowl	[bɔɫ]
ebola	[ibɔ-lə]
love	[lʌv]
polka	[pɔɫ-kə]

In English an onset can consist of a cluster of consonants: /bl/, /pr/, /fl/, /sp/, /tr/, and so on. And English is among a small group of languages that allows certain three-sound combinations to occur

```
              striŋz/
           /        \
       onset         rime
        |          /      \
       str    nucleus     coda
                |          |
                i          ŋz
```

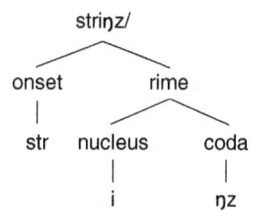

Figure 3.4

as the onset of a syllable in English: /str/, /spl/, /spr/, and /skr/ as in *splash* or *strings*, as illustrated in Figure 3.4.

However, in Maori and Japanese, for example, an onset can have only a single consonant and a rime must be just a vowel; there are no codas (though Japanese can have an /n/). The structure of the syllable in these languages is simply CV, the most common type of syllable in the world's languages. The syllable /ba/, meaning roughly 'place' in Japanese, has the structure shown in Figure 3.5.

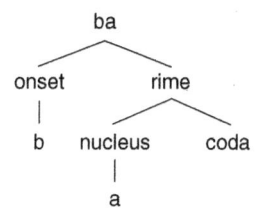

```
              ba
           /      \
       onset      rime
        |       /      \
        b    nucleus   coda
                |
                a
```

Figure 3.5

When a word is borrowed from one language into another, it conforms to the syllable structure of that language. Consider these words in Japanese, which have been borrowed from English; they have been modified—subconsciously—by speakers to conform to the syllable structure of Japanese. The one-syllable English word *strike*, /stɹajk/ becomes a five-syllable Japanese word: su-tu-ra-i-ku. The three-syllable English word *strawberry* becomes a five-syllable Japanese word: su-to-ro-be-ri.

Stress

Another aspect of the study of sound is stress. Stress refers to the relative prominence of certain syllables in a word. This prominence can be achieved in several ways, depending on the language; stress is usually produced by an increase in articulatory force, by an increase in the airflow, and sometimes by increased muscular tension. The results of what we call stress are higher pitch, longer duration, and greater intensity in stressed syllables than in unstressed syllables.

Some languages have predictable and fixed word stress; in Hungarian, Finnish, and Icelandic, for example, stress is always on the first syllable; in Swahili, Polish, and Quechua, the primary stress in a word is always on the next-to-last syllable; in Armenian, stress is on the last syllable of a word. Regular stress patterns such as these then signal word boundaries, so they are relevant for first language acquisition, alerting children to where one word ends and another starts. In other languages, such as English, the position of stress is variable and based on many distinct stress rules (some 43, according to Chomsky and Halle, 1968) that are guided by a variety of phonological and historical factors. For example, Germanic affixes don't affect stress placement; in all of the following; the *earth* syllable is stressed:

éarth   éarthly   unéarthly   unéarthliness

But suffixes on words of Latin do affect stress placement; notice how the stress shifts in these three related words:

grámmar   grammátical   grammaticálity

Stress patterns can vary across dialects of English, so are relevant for those studying language variation:

ínsurance   or   insúrance
pólice   or   políce

Varying the stress can also change the part of speech of a word too. Consider words like *permit*: the noun has stress on the first syllable, while the verb has it on the second. Other examples include the noun-verb pairs *récord and recórd, áddict* and *addíct*, and *óbject* and *objéct*.

Stress correlates with meaning in interesting and patterned ways!

Tone and intonation

Another aspect of the study of phonology is tone, the pitch at which syllables are pronounced. In some languages, such tone shift can make a difference to the meaning of word; in others, even though there may be variation, it conveys no meaning distinction. Tone languages include Thai; some varieties of Chinese; Vietnamese; some languages of Africa such as Yoruba, Zulu, Igbo, and Maninka; and some languages of the Americas including Navajo and Yucatec.

Mandarin Chinese has four tones, illustrated in the following pairs. It is only the differences in tones that result in a meaning distinction.

[mā]   mother   pronounced with a high level tone
[má]   hemp   pronounced with a high rising tone
[mǎ]   horse   pronounced with a low falling rising tone
[mà]   scold   pronounced with a high falling tone

Variation in pitch across a stretch of speech longer than a word is known as **intonation**. Many languages, including English, use such pitch variations to convey surprise or disdain or to denote a question. American English typically has rising intonation across the utterance for questions with a 'yes' or 'no' answer:

Will she ride the bus?
Are you walking home?

Falling intonation is used, however, for *wh*-questions, which were mentioned previously:

> *Where are they going?*
> *How are you getting home?*
> *Which bus will you take?*

Stress and intonation can interact at the sentence level; the word-level stress patterns and pitch can be modified to indicate which part of the sentence is in focus or which word should receive special emphasis. In English, new and important information is typically placed at the end of a clause; therefore, utterance stress, when used neutrally—what we consider a 'normal' intonation contour—is typically associated with the end of the clause. Read the following aloud to hear the 'intonation nucleus,' the syllable that receives the most stress.

> Three dogs were playing in the field.

But change that stressed syllable and see how the meaning changes. Read the following aloud (where the capitalized words are stressed):

> Three DOGS were playing in the field.
> Three dogs were PLAYING in the field.
> Three dogs were playing in the FIELD.

Why study sound?

When you study phonetics—when you describe, categorize, and analyze speech sounds—you are then equipped to do so much with those skills and that knowledge.

- You know how speech sounds are made and how to distinguish among sounds based on their phonetic features.
- You know how and why sounds change over time and that such changes happen in systematic and patterned ways.

- You have acquired a system of transcribing speech using the International Phonetic Alphabet that allows you to record any sound of any spoken language.

And when you study phonology—the sound system of language and the processes underlying it—you then know that:

- There is an intricate subconscious system underlying language; linguistic units are not generally used in isolation, and they work together to make words and sentences.
- Rules also govern pieces bigger than single sounds, including the stress system of words and phrases and the structure of syllables.
- Tone and intonation can affect meaning in systematic ways.

When you study phonetics and phonology, you become more aware of patterns in child language, how sounds are similar and different across languages, how and why accents vary, and how and why language changes. You become aware of how changes in some features which are used to produce certain sounds vary across languages and vary within languages, and how these variations affect not only the meanings of individual words, but also how they correlate with our attitudes towards varieties.

And knowing how sounds are produced and perceived is relevant for speech language pathologists who work with language delays and disorders, for dialect coaches who assist actors, for teaching English to speakers of other languages, for elementary school teachers who can use their knowledge of sounds to understand students' misspellings, and for computational linguists teaching computers to talk. The applications are many and varied.

References

Berko Gleason, J. (1958). The child's learning of English morphology. *Word*, *14*(2–3), 150–177.

Chomsky, N., & Halle, M. (1968). *The sound pattern of English*. Cambridge, MA: MIT Press.

4

The study of words
Morphology

Let's now consider how we study speakers' unconscious knowledge of word structure. In Chapter 2, in the 'Our knowledge of grammar' section, we briefly discussed how our knowledge of word structure, or **morphology**, includes knowledge of **morphemes**, or parts of words, and of **affixation** (suffixes and prefixes in English for example, and the roots and words they attach to). We also have knowledge of **word formation rules** such as *clipping*, *blending*, *backformation*, *compounding*, etc.

As we will see in this chapter, languages don't necessarily share the same morphological rules. Consider, for example, one type of word formation that doubles a part of the word (called **reduplication**) that occurs in Lushootseed, a language of the Pacific Northwest (adapted from Hess & Hilbert, 1995):

ʔálʔal	house	ʔáʔálʔal	hut
ʔúqʷ'ud	pull out	ʔúʔúqʷ'ud	pull part way out
híwil	go ahead	híhíwil	go on ahead a bit
q'íxʷ	upstream	q'íq'íxʷ	a little bit upstream

The first two sounds of a word are doubled in order to make a diminutive: the ʔá of the word for *house* is doubled to make *hut*: ʔáʔálʔal.

As we will also see in this chapter, there is much more to the study of morphology than making words. In fact, the question *What is a word?* is actually quite difficult to answer, because not all languages build words in the same way, yet speakers share some kind of common knowledge that allows them to recognize what is and what is not a possible word in their language.

Morphemes

A morpheme is often described as *the smallest unit of meaning in a word*. This suggests that there are two morphemes in the word *pancake*, namely, *pan* and *cake*, both of which have rather obvious, recognizable meanings, and both of which are words by themselves. Other morphemes have meaning too, though perhaps not in the dictionary sense. English speakers would probably all agree that there are three morphemes in *waspishness* (*wasp*, *-ish*, and *-ness*). We can say that the morphemes *-ish* and *-ness* have meaning because we recognize them as parts of words we easily combine with other parts to create other words, such as *pinkish* and *happiness*. We also know that although *-ish* and *-ness* can attach to adjectives such as *pink* and *happy*, these suffixes can't attach to verbs such as *run* or *work* to create *runnish or *workness. So, although we might have difficulty defining the term *word*, we certainly know what a morpheme is, and we also know a complex set of rules that allow us to combine morphemes to create larger, meaningful units.

Not only are we aware of what a morpheme is, but we also know that there are different types of morphemes. The adjective *pink* is different from the suffix *-ish*; *pink* is a **free morpheme** (it can stand alone as a word) but *-ish* is a **bound morpheme**, one which must be attached to another root or word. And what is a **root**? A root morpheme is the morpheme that remains after all affixes are removed (*sincere* in *insincerity*, or *think* in *unthinkable*).

Words can be **monomorphemic**, or made up of a single morpheme (that may have several syllables), or they can be **polymorphemic**, made up of combinations of morphemes, including **affixes**, such as suffixes and prefixes. *Paper*, *Mississippi*, and *lens* are all monomorphemic as English words, even though we recognize certain parts of them and may be tempted to analyze those as morphemes. For example, *paper* ends in *-er*, which we also find in words such as *taller* and *driver*. But is the *-er* in *paper* the same *-er?* The *-er* in *taller* is a comparative suffix (*tall, taller, tallest*), and the *-er* in *driver* is an agentive suffix, deriving a noun (with the meaning 'one who drives') from the verb *drive*. The *-er* in *paper* is clearly not comparative (*pape, *paper, *papest), nor is it the agentive *-er*, deriving a noun (with the meaning 'one who papes') from a verb *pape*. In *paper*, the *-er* is a bit deceiving; it looks like a suffix but we know it's not; *paper* is monomorphemic. And what about *Mississippi*? For English speakers, this word is monomorphemic, because it can't be broken down into smaller parts (*miss* in this word bears no relation to the English verb (to) *miss* nor to the prefix *mis-* as in *misinformation*). But the name *Mississippi* comes from the Ojibwe phrase *misi-ziibi*, meaning 'Great River.' For Ojibwe speakers, then, this word has two morphemes.

Derivational and inflectional affixation

Affixes themselves can be divided into two different categories. The agentive *-er*, for example, is a **derivational affix**, in this case, a suffix, that derives a new word *driver* from the verb *drive*. To take another example, consider a word like *happiness*; it's made up of a root word, the adjective *happy*, and a derivational suffix, *-ness*, which attaches to adjectives to make nouns. Add a derivational prefix like *un-*, which means something like 'not,' and we have a new word: *unhappiness*. Derivational affixes attach to other morphemes to form new words, what we can think of as separate entries in our mental dictionary, or **lexicon**: *happy*, *happiness*, and *unhappiness* each has its own entry. Other languages have agentive morphemes too. American Sign Language, for example, has an agentive morpheme which turns verbs like TEACH into nouns like TEACHER.

Inflectional affixes do not change the category of the word they attach to, nor do they create new dictionary entries. Instead, they express grammatical information, such as tense, gender, number, case, and other features. English has relatively little inflectional morphology, compared to other more highly inflected languages. In fact, in English there are only eight inflectional affixes, though three of them are the suffix -s, which displays three distinct functions.

Nouns	possessive -s	plural -s		
	Mo's book	books		
Adjectives	comparative -er	superlative -est		
	Mo is tall**er**.	Mo is tall**est**.		
Verbs	3rd person singular	past tense	present participle	past participle
	Mo walk**s**	Mo walk**ed**	Mo is walk**ing**	Mo has walk**ed**
				Mo has eat**en**

In comparison, Old English (OE) was highly inflected. The following comparison of inflectional affixation of the verb *love* provides an example. In Present Day English (PDE), the verb has no inflectional affixation in the present tense except in the third person singular *(loves)*, but in OE there are four distinct suffixes (note also the different forms of the personal pronouns):

Table 4.1 Conjugation of the verb 'love' in PDE and OE

Present Day English	Old English
I love	ic luf**ie**
you love	þu luf**ast**
he/she loves	heo luf**aþ**
we love	we luf**iaþ**
you love	ge luf**iaþ**
they love	hie luf**iaþ**

Although in English, derivational affixes are either prefixes or suffixes, and inflectional affixes are suffixes only, in other languages affixes can be **infixes** and **circumfixes**. In Inuktitut, a language of Western Canada, and a member of the Eskimo-Aleut language family, the infix *-pallia,* inserted after a verb root, adds the meaning roughly translated as 'gradually' to the verb.

nungupjut
'They are disappearing.'

nungup + pallia + jut = nunguppalliajut
'They are disappearing gradually.'

Here is another example of infixation from Tagalog, a language of the Philippines.

bili	'buy'	b-*in*-ili	'bought'
basa	'read'	b-*in*-asa	'read'
sulat	'write'	s-*in*-ulat	'wrote'

The infix -*in*- here is inserted in verbs, after the first consonant of a root, and marks a completed event (something like past tense).

A circumfix (from Latin *circum* 'around') surrounds another morpheme. In German, the circumfix *ge-* + *-t* surrounds the verb root, to create the perfective form of the verb.

| kommen | 'to come' | |
| Er ist gekommt. | 'He has come.' | ge + komm + t |

Expanding inflectional morphology

Not all languages express the same inflectional features. In English, the definite article *the* expresses **definiteness**, picking out a specific member of a set, in contrast to the indefinite article *a*: *I read the book / I read a book*. The indefinite article also expresses **number** (singular – *a book* /*a books), but the definite article is unspecified for number, and can be either singular or plural (*the book/books*). In Arabic, definiteness is marked by a prefix: the noun 'book' *kitāb* is made definite by the prefix *al-* as in *al-kitāb*.

But in other languages, definite and indefinite articles can express other features, such as grammatical **gender**, which is different from biological gender (expressed in words such as *he/she* and in gender-neutral *they*). Language does not necessarily reflect the realities of gender identities, and speech communities come up with other strategies to reflect those identities. Grammatical gender is reflected in the form of a word: in French, *la lune* 'the moon' is feminine, but in German, *der Mond* is masculine, and *das Mädchen*, 'the girl' in German, is neuter. These grammatical gender labels really just indicate different category groupings.

Some languages have two categories, masculine and feminine (Spanish, French, and Celtic and Afro-Asiatic languages), and others distinguish masculine, feminine, and neuter (German, Sanskrit, the Slavic languages). Still others express neuter gender, but masculine and feminine are merged (called *common* gender – Danish and Swedish). Some languages have no grammatical gender at all (Korean, Japanese, various Native American languages, among others). In Ojibwe and other languages, animate nouns have one grammatical gender, and inanimate nouns have another.

Another category that is expressed in some languages morphologically is **animacy**. Most Athabaskan languages, including Navajo, recognize animacy in the grammatical system in various ways; nouns take specific verb forms according to their 'level' of animacy. The Navajo animacy continuum is, according to Young and Morgan (1987):

Human > Infant/Big Animal > Medium-sized Animal > Small Animal > Natural Force > Abstraction

The more animate noun occurs before a lesser animate noun in a sentence; if both nouns are equal in animacy, either one can occur first.

Ashkii at'ééd yiníł'į́
Boy   girl   look
'The boy is looking at the girl.'

But a sentence like the one below is ungrammatical because the less animate noun occurs before the more animate noun:

*Tsídii at'ééd yishtąsh
Bird girl pecked
'The bird pecked at the girl.'

Instead, the word for the girl, *at'ééd*, must precede the word for the bird, *tsídii*, since it precedes it in terms of animacy:

At'ééd tsídii bishtąsh
Bird girl pecked
'The girl was pecked at by the bird.'

The word order as well as the form of the verb (*yishtąsh* compared to *bishtąsh*) conveys that the more animate noun is acting on the less animate noun to perform the action (e.g. 'the girl let herself be pecked by the bird'); thus nouns ranked higher in animacy are more in control. There are interesting interactions here between meaning and world knowledge and syntax and morphological marking.

Case inflection marks a noun's grammatical function. In nominative-accusative languages, the subject of both transitive and intransitive verbs has what grammarians have long called **nominative** case (*she*), and the object of a transitive verb has **accusative** case (*her*).

She saw the man.
NOM

The man saw **her.**   (*see* = transitive)
            ACC

She arrived.   (*arrive* = intransitive)
NOM

Though English expresses case morphologically in its pronoun system (*he/him*, *we/us*, *they/them*), noun phrases do not express nominative or accusative case. *The dog* has the same form, whether as the subject or the object of the verb (*see* – transitive; *bark* – intransitive).

The dog saw the man. **The dog** barked. The man saw **the dog**.

In German and other nominative/accusative case-marking languages, noun phrases do express case; case is expressed by the form of the definite article: *der* is nominative, and *den* is accusative (*der/den* also express gender – masculine, number – singular, and definiteness too).

Der Hund sah den Mann.   **Der Hund** bellte.   Der Mann sah **den Hund**.
NOM   NOM   ACC

In ergative-absolutive languages, such as Dyirbal, an indigenous language of Australia, subjects of transitive verbs have what linguists call **ergative** case, but subjects of intransitive verbs have **absolutive** case, the same case that marks objects of transitive verbs. Other ergative-absolutive languages include Georgian, a Caucasian language; Halkomel'em, a Salish language of the Pacific Northwest; and Mayan, spoken in southern Mexico, Guatemala, Belize, El Salvador, and Honduras. Consider the examples below from Dyirbal (Dixon, 1994, p.160):

Here the noun associated with the intransitive verb has absolutive case (ABS)

ŋuma-Ø   banaga-n^{y}u
father-ABS returned
'Father returned.'

In this next example, 'mother,' the subject of the transitive verb, has ergative (ERG) case marking, but the object 'father' is marked for absolutive case (ABS):

ŋuma-Ø   yabu-ŋgu   buran
father-ABS mother-ERG   saw
'Mother saw father.'

Many languages have far more extensive case systems than either English or German. Estonian has 14 cases, Finnish has 15, and Hungarian, 18!

In some languages, different classes of nouns are associated with different **classifiers**, especially when the noun is accompanied by a number. In Bengali, for example, when counting human nouns one classifier (*-jon*) is used, but when counting non-human nouns, another (*-ṭa*) is used. This classifier (marked CL below) is in the form of a bound morpheme or affix, that attaches to the number word.

Nôe-ṭa ghoṛi
nine-CL clock
'nine clocks'

Ônek-jon lok
many-CL person
'many people'

American Sign Language (ASL) has number morphemes that are bound to words like 'day,' 'week,' and 'year.' Numerical incorporation takes place when you incorporate a number into a sign. For example, instead of signing TWO and then the sign HOUR, you use the TWO handshape as the handshape for your dominant hand while doing the sign for HOUR. Other languages that use classifiers include Chinese, Japanese, Persian, and Mayan, among many others.

Word trees

As we saw in Chapter 3 on the study of phonology, we can graphically represent syllable structure with something like a syllable 'tree.' We can also graphically represent the internal structure of words by using **word trees**. Take *driver* for example; we can

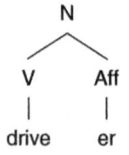

```
         N
        / \
       V   Aff
       |    |
     drive  er
```

Figure 4.1

illustrate its internal structure as shown in Figure 4.1 (where Aff stands for 'affix').

This simple tree allows us to show that *-er* attaches to the verb (V) *drive,* and derives the noun (N) *driver.*

Things get a little more complicated when we consider the noun *unhappiness.* There are two ways we might diagram this word. In Figure 4.2, *un-* attaches to the noun *happiness* (which is formed from *-ness* attaching to the adjective *happy*). In Figure 4.3, *un-* attaches to the adjective *happy*, and then *-ness* attaches to the adjective *unhappy.*

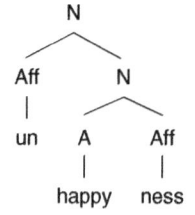

```
        N
       / \
     Aff   N
      |   / \
     un  A   Aff
         |    |
       happy ness
```

Figure 4.2

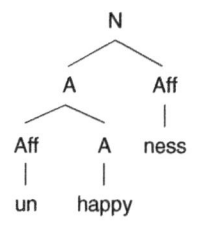

```
         N
        / \
       A   Aff
      / \   |
    Aff  A  ness
     |   |
    un happy
```

Figure 4.3

How do we decide which tree best represents the morphology of this word? The question boils down to whether *un-* attaches to nouns, or to adjectives. We can analyze some additional data to find out.

un- + adjective	un + believable, un + true, un + fortunate, un + decided
un- + noun	*un + shipment, *un + person, *un + escape, *un + threat

These data suggest that *un-* attaches to adjectives but not to nouns, so Figure 4.2 is the correct representation of the internal structure of *unhappiness*. Word trees show us, then, that words don't just have different parts, but that these parts are actually organized into **hierarchical structure**, another aspect of our unconscious knowledge of morphology.

Word trees allow us to express yet another aspect of morphology, namely that inflectional affixes always occur outside of derivational affixes. That is, we have the word *drivers*, where plural *-s* attaches to the noun *driver*, but we never have the opposite order—**driveser*, as shown in Figure 4.4.

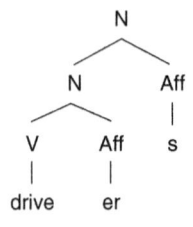

```
            N
           / \
          N   Aff
         / \   |
        V   Aff s
        |   |
      drive er
```

Figure 4.4

Similarly, inflectional affixes on verbs will occur outside of any derivational affixes that are part of the verb. We have *regularizing* but not **regularingize*, as shown in Figure 4.5.

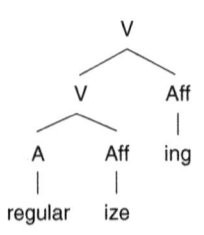

```
            V
           / \
          V   Aff
         / \   |
        A   Aff ing
        |    |
     regular ize
```

Figure 4.5

This makes sense if we think of words in our mental lexicon as including their derivational affixes, and of inflectional affixes as attaching to those words. This is similar to what we find with actual dictionaries; we can look up *driver* and *regularize*, but not *drivers* and *regularizing*. Inflectional affixes do not derive new words nor result in new dictionary entries.

Word trees also help us understand the different meanings of a word or **lexical ambiguity**. To take an example, consider the word *unlockable*. This word is ambiguous—it has more than one meaning.

unlockable 'unable to be locked'
unlockable 'able to be unlocked'

This word has two different meanings, which we can represent in two different word trees in Figures 4.6 and 4.7.

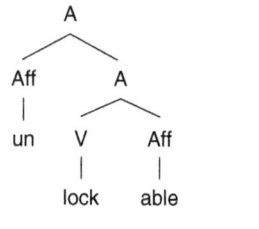

Figure 4.6

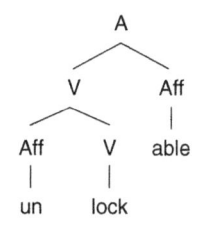

Figure 4.7

There are two distinct *un*-s with different meanings: one which attaches to adjectives and means 'not' (like in *unhappy*) and another which attaches to verbs and mean 'reverse' (as in *untie*, *undo*). The word *unlockable* has two different meanings because it has two different structures.

Types of categories

As you may have noted, the word trees here include labels such as Noun, Verb, Adjective; these are labels of **syntactic categories**, or what you may be more familiar with as **parts of speech**. In fact, the study of morphology is closely tied to the study of syntax, and this overlap is known as **morphosyntax**. We use morphological clues to identify the category of a word; we know that *unlockable* is an adjective because it ends in *able*, and that *drivers* is a noun because it ends in plural *-s*. Morphology intersects with syntax in other ways, which we take up in Chapter 5.

As we mentioned in Chapter 2, we can build new words using different **word formation rules** such as *clipping* (*peeps* from *people*; *totes* from *totally*), *blending* (*jazzercise* from *jazz* and *exercise*), backformation (*liaise* from *liaison*), and so on. Notice that the new words that come into the language are of certain syntactic categories: nouns, verbs, adjectives, adverbs. We call words that fall into the categories N, V, A, and Adv **content words**, or **lexical categories**, because of their contentful meanings. If we look up members of the categories N, V, A, and Adv in a dictionary, we find definitions such as the one for *cat*, given below (from *Merriam-Webster*).

> *Cat: noun*
> a carnivorous mammal (*Felis catus*) long domesticated as a pet and for catching rats and mice

Content words are **open class** words; we can add new words to these categories, and we do so on a regular basis. Here, for example, are some of the candidates for the 2017 American Dialect Society Word of the Year ('fake news' was the winner).

> persisterhood: Blend of 'persist' and 'sisterhood'
> rogue: Describing someone ostensibly working in an administration who is posting messages against it
> shooketh: Mock-archaic way of expressing shock or excitement

stan: Be a big fan (from Eminem song, "Stan")
unicorn: A one-of-a-kind person or thing
askhole: Person who continuously asks ridiculous or obnoxious questions
caucacity: Blend of 'Caucasian' and 'audacity'
alternative facts: Contrary information that matches one's preferred narrative or interpretation of events
avocado toast: A minor indulgence for which people unfairly judge others, especially millennials

But what about words that do not fall into the categories N, V, A, and Adv? What about words like *the* and *very* and *so*, and *and* for that matter? These are all **function words** or **functional categories**, classes of words that express grammatical information (definiteness, case, tense, number, negation, modality, etc., some of which we discussed above), and are defined in the dictionary by what they *do*, rather than by what they mean. Take the entry for the word *the* (emphasis ours) (from *Merriam-Webster*):

the—**used as a function word** to indicate that a following noun or noun equivalent is definite or has been previously specified by context or by circumstance:
'put *the* cat out'

Function words are **closed class** words—we don't add new members to these categories (we don't come up with new determiners or auxiliary verbs at the rapid rate that we add members to open classes of words).

Table 4.2 Content word categories with examples

Noun	Verb	Adjective	Adverb
creek, infatuation, Tokyo, tool, mud, vlog, kitten, hashtag	discuss, remember, annoy, feel, gallop, seem, text	unhappy, important, lovely, sad, tiny, chill, curious	hopefully, fast, still, now, often, achingly

Table 4.3 Function word categories with examples

Determiner	the, a, this, that, those, his, my their, your	Preposition	with, in, on, over, behind, above, around
Numeral	one, five, ten, second, eighth	Conjunction	and, or, yet, for, but, so, nor
Quantifier	all, each, every, both, some	Degree Word	very, so, quite, rather, too
Pronoun	they, he, she, her, theirs, mine, yours	Auxiliary Verb	have, be, do
		Modal	may, might, can, could, will, would, shall, should, must

Not all languages use the same word formation rule nor do they have the exact same inventory of syntactic categories nor the same inventories of lexical and functional categories—though they are very similar. However, all languages seem to have noun-like things and verb-like things, though these categories may not necessarily be identified using the same metrics we apply to determine categories in English and other Indo-European languages.

For example, there is some debate about whether the distinction between nouns and verbs exists in Salish languages, providing an interesting challenge since such categories are generally assumed to exist in all languages. Van Eijk and Hess (1986) suggest that the distinction does exist based on that fact that only some stems can take possessive affixes in several of the languages; Davis and Matthewson (1999), for example, provide evidence from the language St'át'imcets for category distinctions, though more research remains to be done!

Linguists study many other puzzles about word classes or categories across languages; as we saw above, Mandarin, ASL, Japanese, Korean, and other languages, for example, have *classifiers* that express measures and numbers, but Indo-European languages lack this category altogether (and use other strategies to express these concepts). Some languages, such as Hungarian, lack the category preposition, and in others, such as Mohawk or Lushootseed, adjectives and adverbs do not seem to be distinct categories. Still other languages have different categories, or classes, of nouns: in Navajo nouns are classified according to their animacy, shape, and consistency. In the Australian aboriginal language Dyirbal, nouns fall into four different classes: (1) animate objects, men; (2) women, water, fire, violence; (3) edible fruit and vegetables; and (4) nouns not classified by the first three criteria.

Morphological typologies

As we mentioned above, English has very few inflectional affixes (only eight). Other languages have many more, and some languages have no inflections at all, and express that grammatical information through full words, rather than affixes. Such languages are called **analytic** languages. Consider Chinese, where the word *le* is used to convey various aspects of time. In the examples below, the translation suggests past tense, but it can convey other aspects of time as well. Distinct from synthetic languages, though, the *le* stands alone, rather than being a part of the verb.

> Tā mǎi le   yī gè   xīn shǒujī.
> He buy LE a new cell phone
> 'He bought a new cell phone.'

> Tamen ge   chi le   san   ge pingguo
> They   each eat LE   three-CL apple
> 'They each ate three apples.'

In Chapter 2, we mentioned pidgin and creole languages, which have little if any inflectional morphology. These languages are also largely analytic, and use words, rather than affixes, to express inflection. We illustrate here with examples from African American English, which some have argued is a creole. Regardless of its origins, the AAE tense and aspect system is analytic, expressing inflection with words (*be*, *bin*, and *been*) rather than affixes. (Examples adapted from Rickford, 1999.)

Habitual *be:* She *be* runnin.
(*She is usually running/would be running:* habitual aspect)

Unstressed *been/bin*: She *been/bin* married.
(*She has been married at some earlier point:* present perfect but not remote)

Stressed *BEEN/BIN:* She *BEEN/BIN* married.
(*She has been married for a long time and still is*: remote past)

As these examples illustrate, the various forms of the verb *be* express grammatical information that other varieties of English express with different combinations of the auxiliary verbs *have* and *be* and/or with adverbs like *usually* and phrases such a *for a long time / a long time ago.*

In contrast to analytic languages like Vietnamese and English, **synthetic** languages express inflection with affixation, rather than with separate words. For example, English expresses future tense by adding the modal verb *will* to a sentence, but Spanish and other Romance languages express future tense through affixation.

Habl<u>o</u>   I speak.   -*o* = first person, singular, present tense
Habl<u>aré</u>   I will speak.   -*aré* = first person, singular, future tense

Languages that have a high number of morphemes per word are called **polysynthetic** languages. An example is Swahili; the word *utawapenda* is a whole sentence in its English translation, but is a single Swahili word:

u-ta-wa-penda
you-FUTURE-them-like
'You will like them.'

Another example of a polysynthetic language is Yup'ik, spoken in parts of Alaska and Russia:

kaipiallrulliniuk
kaig-pirar-llru-llini-u-k
be.hungry-really-PAST-apparently-INDICATIVE-they.two
'The two of them are apparently really hungry.'
(Mithun, 1999)

But how do we know that *kaipiallrulliniuk*, for example, is a single word since it seems to convey the same meaning as an entire sentence in English? This brings us back the question that linguists aim to answer: what is a word?

What is a word?

Words can be identified in several ways. Some definitions apply across languages, and others are more language-specific. The best criterion is usually the judgment of native speakers. Whether or not they have given much thought to grammar, speakers of most languages can repeat a sentence word-by-word with confidence, pausing between words. In natural speech, speakers seldom pause in the middle of words; if they are interrupted mid-word, they generally start anew, returning to the beginning of the word. Speakers are usually aware of the meanings of whole words, but they are often not conscious of the meanings of individual morphemes within the word nor of the boundaries between these.

Words can often be identified in particular languages by other specific characteristics as well. Words have no more than one primary stress, and in some languages, stress regularly occurs on a specific syllable. In the language isolate Chitimacha, spoken in Louisiana, the main stress always occurs on the first syllable of a word; in Tuscarora, spoken in North Carolina, New York, and Ontario, it occurs on the next-to-last syllable. (You can see how the study of morphology interacts with both the study of phonology and of syntax.)

Studying the structure of polysynthetic and non-polysynthetic languages involves trying to understand what a word is, which is also important even for a more analytic language like English.

Words in some languages are easily identified by their morphological structure. Yup'ik verbs always begin with a root morpheme and always end with a pronoun.

There are other cases in which boundaries between certain words are less clear. Sometimes this is because adjacent words can fuse gradually over time. We can see how this has happened even in the writing system with compound words in English like *high chair* becoming *highchair*, and we also see it when words change into what we call **clitics**, which are sort of between words and affixes, such as the *n't* in *don't, can't, won't*. Other examples of clitics in English include *-s* in *he's leaving* or *she's not home*, and the reduced form of infinitival *to* that attaches to a previous verb: *gonna, wanna, supposta*, etc. Romance languages have complex clitic pronouns, as illustrated with an example below from Spanish, where the two clitic pronouns attach to the verb.

    dámelo
    dá + me + lo
    give me   it
    'Give it to me.'

Is dámelo a single word? Are *don't* and *gonna*? We can see from these examples from diverse languages that although we might think, initially, that the question *What is a word?* is easy to answer, its answer is actually quite complex, and part of a rich area of ongoing research in linguistics.

Why study words?

When we study morphology—words and their parts—we learn how to analyze and describe words and their parts, and we gain a deeper understanding of the different rule systems that underlie how words are structured across languages.

- You can identify different types of morphemes, including roots and affixes.

- You are aware of the complexity of defining the notion 'word,' given different languages' morphological typologies (synthetic, analytic, polysynthetic).
- You know about word formation processes that we use to create new words.
- You have acquired some tools of morphological analysis that help us identify the syntactic category of a word.

As the study of phonetics and phonology reveals as well, the study of morphology reveals a great deal about language acquisition, change, and variation. Morphological study makes us aware of how children create words and apply morphological rules as they progress through stages of language acquisition. And we distinguish one language variety from another not only by their different phonological rules (accents), but also by their different morphological rules and lexicons, or vocabularies. Morphological rules also change over time, and morphological change is an important area of study in historical linguistics. Understanding word structure is important for lexicographers (dictionary-makers) who not only catalog new words that come into the language but who study etymology, or the origins of words; for foreign language teaching; for product naming. Knowledge of morphology is also essential for literacy education, and words and their structure are fundamental in writing, from poetry to technical writing.

References

Davis, H., & Matthewson, L. (1999). On the functional determination of lexical categories. *Revue québécoise de linguistique, 27*, 30–69.

Dixon, R.M.W. (1994). *Ergativity*. Cambridge, England: Cambridge University Press.

Van Eijk, J.P., & Hess, T. (1986). Noun and verb in Salish. *Lingua, 69*(4), 319–331.

Hess, T., & Hilbert, V. (1995). *Lushootseed grammar book 1: The language of the Skagit, Nisqually, and other tribes of Puget Sound*. Seattle, WA: Lushootseed Press.

Mithun, M. (1999) *The languages of Native North America.* Cambridge, UK: Cambridge University Press.

Rickford, J.R. (1999) *African American Vernacular English.* Oxford, UK: Blackwell.

Young, R., & Morgan, W. (1987) *The Navajo language: A grammar and colloquial dictionary.* Albuquerque, NM: University of New Mexico Press.

5

The study of sentence structure

Syntax

Like the question *What is a word?* the question *What is a sentence?* is difficult to answer. We have seen that, regardless of the language we speak, we know, unconsciously, what a word is and what parts of words are. We have also seen that in some languages, namely polysynthetic languages, a word can actually be an entire sentence. The study of sentence structure, or **syntax**, therefore overlaps in crucial ways with the study of word structure, or morphology, or the study of **morphosyntax**. In this chapter, we will take a look at what linguists study when they study syntax, and along the way we will see how the study of syntax often overlaps with the study of morphology and other components of grammar.

Revisiting syntactic categories

In the previous chapter we discussed how words fall into two basic categories, *lexical* and *functional* categories. Morphology provides us with clues to the category of a word; we know that *serenity* is a noun because it is affixed by *-ity*, a derivational affix that makes nouns out of adjectives. Syntax also provides us with clues to the category of a word.

From your early days in school you may have learned that a *noun* is 'a person, place or thing,' and a verb is 'the action' in the sentence. These are meaning-based definitions of parts of speech, and though useful to some extent, they do not really capture our knowledge of syntactic categories. For example, consider the following sentence:

There was a fight.

Here, the 'action' of the sentence is expressed by the noun *fight*, and the verb, *was*, expresses, well, what? Not really anything at all, yet we know it is a verb because of its position, between the subject and the object. In fact, we can easily pick out nouns and verbs in a nonsense sentence like the one below, even if we don't have any idea what they mean.

The epax veeled a tormi.

In this sentence, we know that *epax* and *tormi* are nouns, and *veeled* is a verb, even though these nonsense words have no recognizable meanings. How do we know, then, the categories of these words?

In an analytic language like English, which does not have much inflectional affixation, the position of a word in the sentence provides us with important clues to its syntactic category. Because English is an SVO language (subject-verb-object), we know that *epax* is a noun in our nonsense sentence because it occurs after *the*, and before the verb, *veeled*. We know that *veeled* is a verb in part because it is affixed with the past tense suffix -*ed*, but also because of its position, after the subject *the epax* and before the object *a tormi*. We know that *tormi* is a noun because of its position after the article *a*, and because it occurs in the object position after the verb *veeled*.

Now consider this sentence:

We epax at least four times a day.

What is the category of *epax* here? It has the same form as the noun *epax* in the previous sentence, but it is now in a different syntactic position, where we expect verbs, not nouns. So even though we again have no idea what *epax* means, our knowledge of syntax tells us that it is a verb here, not a noun. Notice too, that morphology provides us with no clues here; there is no recognizable derivational or inflectional morphology on *epax* to help us determine its category.

Linguists who study syntax endeavor to discover the underlying rules that govern word order in a particular language and across languages. All languages have syntax, and all have categories, but as we briefly discussed in Chapter 4, not always the same ones.

Phrase structure

In addition to studying how words fall into different syntactic categories, linguists also study **phrase structure**, or how words are grouped together into larger syntactic units. For example, if you were asked to break the following sentence into two main groups of words, you would most likely do it like this:

[The grey kitten] [unrolled a ball of yarn]

But not this:

[The grey] [kitten unrolled a ball of yarn]

And certainly not this:

[The grey kitten unrolled a] [ball of yarn]

Our unconscious knowledge of syntax therefore includes the knowledge that certain groups of words function as units, or **phrases**, within the larger unit, the **clause** (which is different from a sentence, but we'll get to that later!).

Native speakers of a language can not only identify different phrases in a clause, they can also identify the main word, or **head**, of each part, or phrase. For example, English speakers know that the noun *kitten* heads a noun phrase, or NP, and the verb *unrolled* heads a verb phrase, or VP, and so on. Moreover, speakers of a language know what is a possible phrase in their language and what is not. We can provide **phrase structure rules** for English sentence structure that capture the basic structure of each phrase. Parentheses indicate something that is optional. (Actual phrase structure rules are far more complex than what we are providing here, and phrase structure is a topic of much research in syntax.)

```
S → NP VP
VP → V NP
NP → Det (AP) N (PP)
PP → P NP
AP → A
```

According to these basic (and incomplete) phrase structure rules, the clause (S 'sentence') is made up of two parts, a noun phrase (NP) subject and a verb phrase (VP) predicate. The VP includes a verb and its NP object. NP includes a determiner (*the/a*), an optional adjective phrase, a head N, and an optional prepositional phrase (PP). PP includes a head P and an object NP, and AP includes a head A.

Using these rules, we can draw a **phrase structure tree** like the one in Figure 5.1 for our 'kitten' sentence. (A question that arises in research on syntax is whether all languages have phrase structure in the way we have described for English. We address this below in the section *Morphosyntax*.)

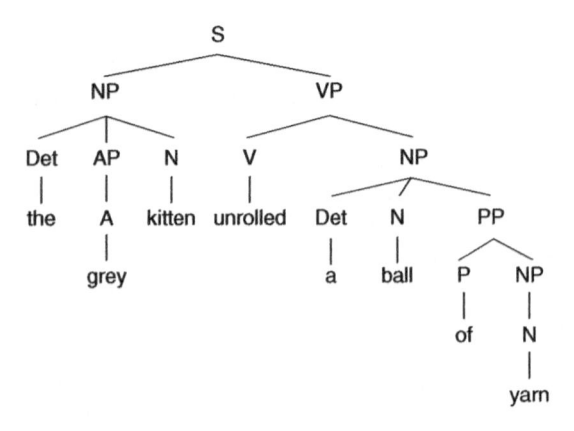

Figure 5.1

Hierarchical structure and recursion

The tree in Figure 5.1 helps us illustrate a number of things about syntactic structure. Not only can we identify *heads* and *phrases*, and their *syntactic categories*, we can also capture the fact that phrase structure is **hierarchical**. That is, one phrase can be included in another phrase; the PP *of yarn* is included in the larger NP *a ball of yarn*, which is included in the larger VP *unrolled a ball of yarn* and so on. Phrase structure trees allow us to demonstrate that sentences are not simply strings of words in linear order; they are organized hierarchically, into units within other units.

This tree allows us to illustrate yet another interesting property of syntactic structure, namely **recursion**, the property of phrase structure rules that enables the generation of phrases of infinite length. Recursion is much easier to illustrate than to explain! Consider, for example, the phrase structure rules for NP and PP in English, repeated below.

NP → Det (AP) N (**PP**)
PP → P **NP**

According to these two phrase structure rules, an NP can include a PP that in turn includes an NP (that can include a PP that includes an NP....and so on). In other words, these rules illustrate how we can build, or **generate**, an NP that includes another NP, as illustrated in Figure 5.2.

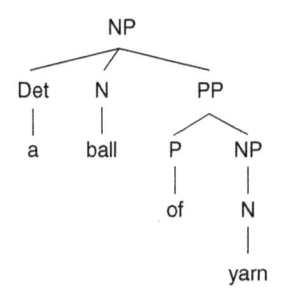

Figure 5.2

But we don't need to stop there; these rules actually allow us to generate NPs of *infinite* length. Here's an example of recursion from a traditional children's song that you may be familiar with:

There's a hole in the bottom of the sea
There's a log in the hole in the bottom of the sea
There's a bump on a log in a hole in the bottom of the sea
There's a frog on a bump on a log in a hole in the bottom of the sea

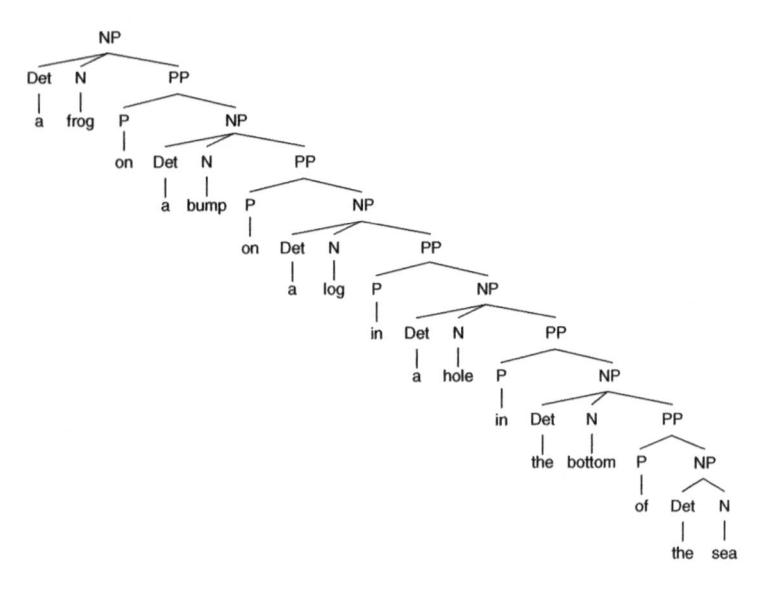

Figure 5.3

Recursion, and the hierarchical syntactic structure that recursive phrase structure rules give rise to, appears to be a property that all languages share. Interestingly, even though syntactic rules are recursive, our memories can only process so much, and keep us from producing incredibly long utterances.

Syntactic ambiguity

What else do we know about syntax? In earlier sections we introduced **lexical** and **syntactic** ambiguity, or how words and sentences can have more than one meaning. Recall that the word *unlockable* is lexically ambiguous, and the phrase *English cotton shirts* is also ambiguous, but not because of any ambiguous word. Rather, this phrase is **syntactically ambiguous**: it has two different syntactic structures; hence, two different meanings.

[English [cotton shirts]]   [[English cotton] shirts]

Our intuitive knowledge of syntax allows us to understand ambiguous sentences and to then make hypotheses about what that ambiguity stems from. Consider this sentence:

The linguist studied the language with a few native speakers.

Any native English speaker recognizes that this sentence is ambiguous; either the linguist studied a language that itself has a few native speakers, or the linguist studied a language, perhaps with the help of a few native speakers.

In Figure 5.4, *the language with a few native speakers* forms a single unit, or noun phrase. We can even replace the NP *the*

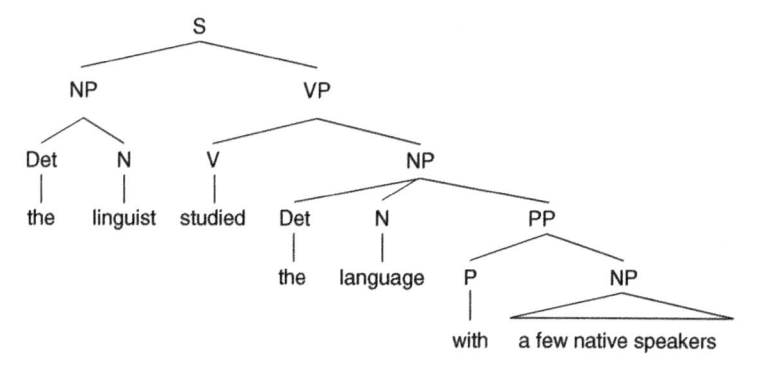

Figure 5.4

language with a few native speakers with the name of the language, say, Squamish, a language of the Pacific Northwest. We can paraphrase this sentence as *The linguist studied Squamish (a language with a few native speakers)*.

In the next tree, Figure 5.5, the NP *the language* does *not* include the PP *with a few native speakers*.

```
                          S
              ┌───────────┴───────────┐
             NP                      VP
            ╱  ╲          ┌───────────┼───────────┐
          Det   N         V          NP          PP
           │    │         │        ╱   ╲        ╱  ╲
          the linguist studied   Det    N      P    NP
                                  │     │      │    ╱╲
                                 the language with  a few native speakers
```

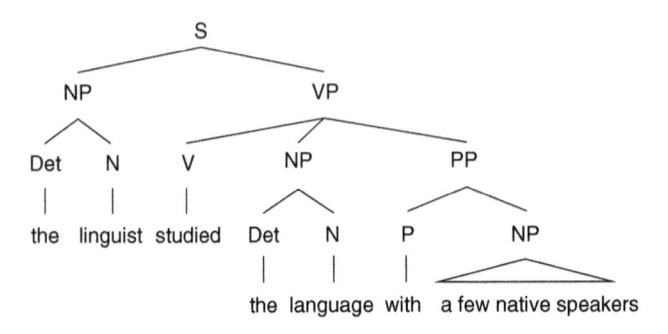

Figure 5.5

We can paraphrase this sentence as *The linguist studied Squamish, along with/with the assistance of a few native speakers.* Understanding phrase structure therefore provides us with insights into how sentences are organized, and how this organization can affect meaning.

Syntactic typologies

Just as we can classify languages by their different morphological typologies, we can classify languages by their different **syntactic typologies**, or basic word orders. So far, we have discussed only the phrase structure of English, a language that has a base order of SVO (subject-verb-object). But of course not all languages are SVO like English, Mandarin, and Zulu; others, such as German and Japanese are SOV, and still others, such as Irish, Arabic and Hawaiian are VSO. A few languages (Apalaí, Hixkaryana) have OVS word order, but this order is quite rare.

Recall that the phrase structure rule for an English clause (S) is the following, meaning that a sentence is made up of a NP and a VP:

S → NP VP

SOV languages have this same basic structure, but by simply 'flipping' the order of V and NP in VP, we achieve the appropriate word order: Figure 5.6 is the tree diagram for the following German sentence.

Lee hat das Buch gelesen
Lee has the book read
'Lee read the book.'

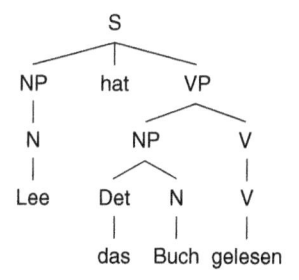

```
              S
        ___|___
    NP    hat    VP
    |          _____
    N         NP     V
    |        __|     |
   Lee     Det  N    V
            |   |    |
           das Buch gelesen
```

Figure 5.6

Japanese, which shares SOV word order, would have this same word order.

We can diagram OVS order by assuming that instead of NP + VP order, the language has VP + NP order. Here is an example from Hixkaryana, a Carib language spoken in Brazil (example from Derbyshire, 1985; 3SG = 3rd person singular, DISTPST = distant past, COMPL = completive).

Toto   yo-no-ye   kamara
person   3SG-eat-DISTPST.COMPL   jaguar
'The jaguar ate the man.'

```
          S
         / \
        VP   NP
       / \    |
      NP  V   N
      |   |   |
      N yonoye kamara
      |
     toto
```

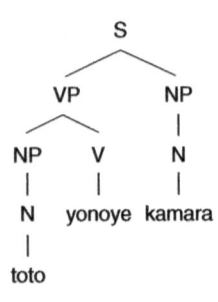

Figure 5.7

But, it is not as obvious how to represent the structure of languages with VSO word order. Here is an example from Welsh (O'Grady, Archibald, Aronoff, & Rees-Miller, 2017):

Lladdodd y   ddraig   y   dyn.
killed   the dragon the man
'The dragon killed the man.'

Whether we assume that within the clause the order is [NP VP] or [VP NP], our phrase structure rules alone fail to explain how languages end up with VSO order, where the subject occurs *between* the verb and its object. The possible orders we can account for are diagrammed below in Figures 5.8–5.11.

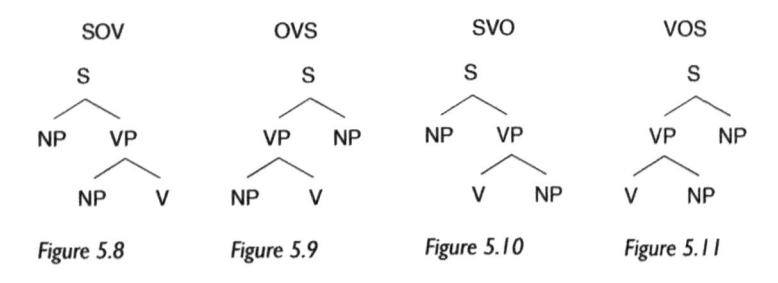

SOV   OVS   SVO   VOS

```
    S             S             S              S
   / \           / \           / \            / \
  NP  VP        VP  NP        NP  VP         VP  NP
     / \      / \                / \        / \
    NP  V   NP   V              V   NP     V   NP
```

Figure 5.8   *Figure 5.9*   *Figure 5.10*   *Figure 5.11*

In the following section we pursue this question of the derivation of VSO order, which can't be answered simply in terms of phrase structure. We need to instead turn to another aspect of research in syntax, *movement*.

Movement

A great deal of research on syntactic structure involves attempting to explain how word order can be rearranged in different languages under certain conditions (we briefly introduced some examples of movement in Chapter 2 in the section "How do we study language scientifically?"). For example, although English is a SVO language, speakers often produce sentences that aren't SVO. When we form questions, for example, we might argue that word order is VSO, because the verb *is* occurs in sentence-initial position.

> The student **is** happy.
> **Is** the student happy?

To take another example, recall that in English *wh*-questions, an interrogative phrase such as *who*, *what*, *where*, etc. occurs in sentence-initial position. In the following example, the object of the verb, *what*, occurs in this position. Does this mean that English is an OSV language?

> The student has bought **something**.
> **What** has the student bought ____?

And let's take one more example. Even if unfamiliar with the terminology, English speakers know how to take an *active* sentence:

> The student bought a bicycle.

And make it *passive*:

> A bicycle was bought by the student.

In the passive sentence, the subject *the student* occurs at the end of the sentence, and the object *a bicycle* occurs in the subject position.

How do we account for these different orders in English? Put slightly differently, what do English speakers have to know about syntax in order to rearrange words and phrases in the ways possible in their language? And as with any research in linguistics, the next question is, what about other languages? Do the same reordering phenomena appear, and if so, why, and if not, why not?

The phenomenon in question here is called **movement**, a simple name for a complex system of rules that account for how speakers of a language can rearrange words in that language. Movement rules account for the possible orders in a language that differ from the base order; movement is involved in forming what are called *yes/no-* and *wh-*questions in English, and in forming a passive sentence from an active one.

Movement rules exist across languages, and studying them reveals what languages seem to have in common, and how they differ. Compare more English questions with similar questions in French. To form questions in sentences with an auxiliary and a main verb in English, just the auxiliary verb moves to sentence-initial position:

She has bought a bicycle   →   **Has** she bought a bicycle?

But when no auxiliary is present (and the verb is not a form of *be*), we use auxiliary *do* to form questions.

She bought a bicycle   →   **Did** she buy a bicycle?
(instead of moving just the verb: ***Bought** she a bicycle?)

In French questions, the auxiliary verb, if there is one, moves to sentence-initial position just as in English.

Elle **a** acheté un vélo.   →   **A**-t-elle acheté un vélo?
She has bought a bicycle   Has-t-she bought a bicycle
'She has bought a bicycle?'   'Has she bought a bicycle?'

But in the absence of an auxiliary verb, the main verb moves to this position. (French has no equivalent of *do* to use in questions.)

Elle **achète** un vélo.	→	**Achète**-t-elle un vélo?
She buys a bicycle		Buys-t-she a bicycle
'She buys a bicycle.'		'Did she buy a bicycle?'

This small set of data suggests that both English and French have **verb movement**, but the rule operates slightly differently in each language. The linguist constructing a theory of syntax would attempt to account for this difference, examining data involving verb movement in English and French and other languages.

Research on verb movement reveals a possible answer to the word order conundrum we posed above, namely how to account for VSO order in languages like Irish and Welsh. If we propose that the base order in these and other VSO languages is actually SVO, but that unlike in other SVO languages, verb movement in VSO languages to sentence-initial position is obligatory, then the VSO order is explained.

The Welsh sentence below:

Lladdodd y ddraig y dyn.
killed the dragon the man
'The dragon killed the man.'

is, therefore, according to this analysis, derived by applying verb movement to the base order below, as shown in the movement deriving the tree in Figure 5.13 from the one in Figure 5.12:

y ddraig lladdodd y dyn.
the dragon killed the man
'The dragon killed the man.'

Movement rules not only allow us to explain deviations from base word orders within and across languages, but they also illustrate an important aspect of our syntactic knowledge.

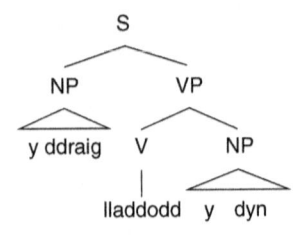

Figure 5.12

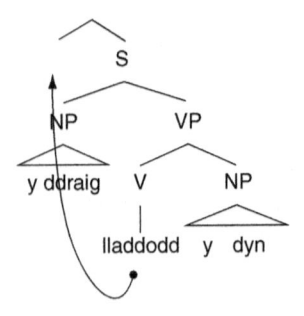

Figure 5.13

Deletion

There are many other syntactic phenomena, in addition to phrase structure and movement, that linguists study. A topic of much research in syntax is **deletion** (also called **ellipsis**), the process by which syntactic material is omitted, but nevertheless clearly understood. Consider, for example, the following:

> I bought six books but you bought only two.
> Lee is going to the movies tonight but Cary isn't.

What's missing here? We know that in the first sentence, Cary bought only two books (not, for example, two pizzas or two apples, etc.). In the second sentence, we know that Cary isn't going to the movies, and this is the only interpretation of what Cary isn't doing. This may seem unremarkable, but in fact, how do we explain that we have these very precise and uncontroversial interpretations of these sentences?

Linguists propose that in these sentences, a deletion operation has taken place; material is not only deleted, but **deleted under identity** with some preceding material.

> Lee bought six books but Cary bought only two ~~books~~.
> Lee is going to the movies tonight but Cary isn't ~~going to the movies~~.

Deletion under identity ensures that only identical material will be deleted, and thus explains why our interpretations of the meanings of such sentences is neither random nor arbitrary. Rather, our interpretations follow from a very precise syntactic rule.

We can think about the concepts we have talked about here, including phrase structure rules, recursion, hierarchical structure, movement and deletion rules as part of our mental grammar, an unconscious computational system that allows us to produce and understand any sentence in our language, even ones we have never heard before.

Morphosyntax

Recall from the introduction to this section that morphology and syntax overlap in a number of ways, and that this area of study is called **morphosyntax**. One simple example of morphosyntax is illustrated by **subject-verb agreement**. In many varieties of English, the morphology on the verb depends on the syntactic subject that precedes it.

> he/she/it **walks** to school.   I/they/you/we **walk** to school.

In some languages, the morphological agreement on the verb (of person, number, and tense) allows speakers to omit the subject altogether, perhaps because the relevant information (of person, number) can be recovered from verb agreement. Such languages are called **null subject languages**. Hebrew, Japanese, Korean, Punjabi, and many other languages are null subject languages, and we illustrate here with an example from Italian.

> Maria non vuole mangiare.   Non vuole mangiare.
> Maria not wants to-eat   (he/she) not wants to eat
> 'Maria doesn't want to eat.' '(he/she) doesn't want to eat'

Recall from the previous chapter on morphology that languages can be divided into different morphological classes, or typologies. **Analytic** languages express grammatical inflection with single words, and typically rely on word order to express other grammatical relations such as subject, object, etc. **Synthetic** languages express inflections with affixes, and can have somewhat more flexible word order than analytic languages. Languages that have a high number of morphemes per word are called **polysynthetic** languages; in these languages, nearly all grammatical relationships are expressed by morphemes attached to the verb. We gave an example from Swahili, repeated here. The word *utawapenda* is a whole sentence in its English translation, but is a single Swahili word:

> u-ta-wa-penda
> you-FUTURE-them-like
> 'You will like them.'

Another example we discussed was from Yup'ik, spoken in parts of Alaska and Russia. Again, you can see that in this language, a sentence is a single word:

> kaipiallrulliniuk
> kaig-pirar-llru-llini-u-k
> be.hungry-really-PAST-apparently-INDICATIVE-they.two
> 'The two of them are apparently really hungry.'

How do polysynthetic languages fit into the model of syntax that we have described so far? Can we draw tree diagrams for sentences/words in polysynthetic languages? How do we describe the syntactic structure of such languages, where a sentence can also be defined as a word? Research on polysynthetic and agglutinating languages reveals that there is indeed evidence for phrase structure in such languages, and that research on the diverse morphosyntax of polysynthetic languages provides us with insights that one might otherwise miss. Consider the following two sentences from Mohawk (Baker, 2001).

> Ranhuwe's.
> likes
> 'He likes it.'

> Atya'tawi   Sak   ranhuwe's.
> dress   Sak   likes
> 'Sak likes the dress.'

In Mohawk, the verb alone, *Ranhuwe's*, fulfills the core requirements for a complete sentence. Baker proposes the tree presented in Figure 5.14 for the second sentence, where the two NPs simply add additional information.

Hierarchical structural relationships and basic syntactic relationships hold in Mohawk, as in English, French, or Japanese,

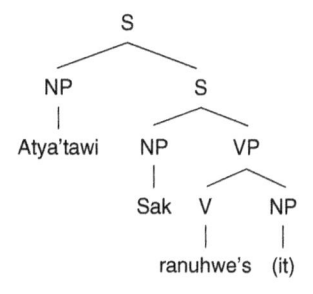

```
              S
            /   \
          NP     S
          |    /   \
       Atya'tawi NP   VP
                |   /   \
               Sak V    NP
                   |     |
               ranuhwe's (it)
```

Figure 5.14

but the structure differs slightly. Just as the study of morphology strives to answer the question *What is a word?* the study of syntax leads us to wonder about and investigate the question *What is a sentence?*

Why study sentence structure?

When you study syntax, or sentence structure, you learn that sentences are far more than linear strings of words. The study of syntax, like the study of any other component of grammar, provides us with insights into our 'mental grammar' and the system of unconscious grammatical rules that allow us to produce and understand sentences in a language. It also helps us understand that differences among languages may be superficial; though Irish, Hixkaryana, English, Mohawk, and other languages might look quite different on the surface, we find, when we understand more about how syntax works and how it intersects with morphology, that these difference aren't so mysterious after all.

- You understand, based on your own linguistic intuitions, that words fall into different syntactic categories, based on their position in the sentence.
- You also learn that words are organized into larger units, or phrases, each of which has a head.
- You learn that sentence structure has certain properties, including phrase structure rules, recursion, hierarchical structure, and deletion rules.
- You understand that the syntactic operation of movement allows us to account for variations in word order within and across languages.
- You discover the relationship between morphology and syntax, and how these two components of grammar overlap.

When you study syntax, you can see how children progress through different stages of acquisition, as their syntax gets progressively more complex. You can also see how languages change syntactically over time; Old English word order is quite different from that of Present Day English, and Middle English has different word order still. You can identify different syntactic patterns in different language varieties, patterns that distinguish one dialect from another. Knowledge of syntax is useful in many ways. It is useful to those who study bilingualism and code-switching, and to those who work in bilingual education, or who teach language arts or world languages. Knowledge of syntax is fundamental to coding and computer programming (Siri needs syntax!) and to studying language disorders and aphasia, among many other applications.

References

Baker, M. (2001). *The atoms of language: The mind's hidden rules of grammar*. New York, NY: Basic Books.

Derbyshire, D. (1985). *Hixkaryana and linguistic typology*. Summer Institute of Linguistics. Arlington, Texas: University of Texas at Arlington.

O'Grady, W., Archibald, J., Aronoff, M., & Rees-Miller, J. (2017). *Contemporary linguistics: An introduction*. New York, NY: MacMillan.

6

The study of meaning
Semantics and pragmatics

In Chapter 1, we introduced some semantic concepts to help illustrate our unconscious knowledge of meaning. We briefly discussed *ambiguity*, *entailment*, and *quantifier scope*, to show that our knowledge of meaning goes far beyond understanding the meanings of words. Here, we will provide some more examples of the kinds of phenomena that linguists study when they study word and sentence meaning, or **semantics**. In addition to semantics, linguists also study conversational interactions and how we convey meaning in certain contexts. The study of meaning in context is called **pragmatics**, and we provide some examples of topics linguists might study in this area as well.

Semantic relationships among words

We all learn about the *-nyms* in school: homonyms, synonyms, antonyms, and more. We think of these relationships as fairly obvious and easy to explain; synonyms are words that mean the same thing, and antonyms are words that have opposite meanings. But these meaning relationships are actually quite a bit more complex, and the topic of much investigation in linguistics.

Take **synonyms** for the adjective *angry*, for example. We might think of *furious, mad, irate, wrathful* as synonyms. But do these adjectives all mean exactly the same thing? In fact, linguists argue that synonyms usually differ in meaning in what may be subtle ways. If you are *angry* are you also *furious? Wrathful?* Is *mad* a closer match to *angry* than these other adjectives? Why/why not? We can imagine a child being *talkative*, but perhaps not *verbose*, even if the two words seem synonymous. **Antonymy** is similarly complex. In terms of the physics of light and the color spectrum, *black* and *white* might be considered exact antonyms, or opposites. But what about *hot* and *cold*? Are these antonyms? You can imagine that not all of us would agree on what we consider *hot* coffee, nor on what outdoor temperature we consider to be *cold*. And we also think of pairs like *mother-daughter* and *doctor-patient* as antonyms, and what about *salt* and *pepper?!* **Polysemy** is another complex semantic relationship among words; polysemous words have related meanings. *Foot*, for example, can mean your physical foot, or the foot of bed, of the foot of a mountain, or even a measurement. Polysemous words are therefore different from **homophonous** words, or words that sound the same but have unrelated meanings, and same or different spellings. *Bat/bat* (a vampire bat/a baseball bat) are homophones, as are *flour/flower* and *pen/pen* (the noun and the verb), and so one. Homophony and polysemy give rise to lexical **ambiguity**: words that can have more than one meaning.

Given all these complex semantic relationships among words, is it possible to even define what 'meaning' is? Think about the word *dog*. Native English speakers would likely all agree that the noun *dog* refers to a four-legged canine. But even though we might understand the **denotation** of the word *dog* (as referring to a member of the set of animals we agree to be dogs), the word *dog* may have different **connotations**, or associations, for each of us. Both denotation and connotation make up the meaning of a word, but neither can account for a word's meaning by itself. Think, too, about concepts such as *mountain* or *hot*; we agree, on some level, on what each of these words means, though what, in reality, a mountain is to someone who lives in the Rocky Mountains of Montana is different from what someone in Appalachia considers a mountain.

Metaphor and figurative language

The study of **metaphor** also delves into the complex interaction between semantics and how we conceptualize the world.

Metaphors describe one thing in terms of another, usually with some (possibly hidden) similarity. For example, the well-known phrase *Love is a rose* works as a metaphor because it equates love with a symbol of beauty and possible pain, a rose. *Love is a chair*, on the other hand, doesn't really work as a metaphor, because there is no obvious connection in meaning between the emotion of love and a piece of furniture. But metaphors are far more complex than this example suggests. Consider, for example, how we use the metaphor *argument as war*:

> Your claims are indefensible.
> You attacked every point in my argument.
> I've never won an argument with you.
> You shot down all my arguments.

Lakoff and Johnson (1980) argue that metaphors are not arbitrary, but rather are connected to how we see the world, to our mental *conceptual structures*. Contemporary American English metaphors about time, they would argue, reflect our cultural perceptions. *Time is money*: we invest it, budget it, waste it, spend it, save it, don't have it, and lose it. Cross-linguistic studies of metaphors and other figurative language are a rich area of study that can lead us to a better understanding of how language does or does not reflect shared conceptual structures.

Here are some other examples of figurative language:

Metonymy: describing something in terms of something with which it is closely associated. *The pen* can refer to writing or diplomacy, and *the sword* to war or violence.

The pen is mightier than the sword.

Synesthesia: one kind of sensation is described in terms of another. Poet Charles Baudelaire, in *Correspondences*, describes 'perfumes' (smells) in terms of touch (fresh like the skin of infants), sound (sweet like oboes), and color (green like prairies).

There are perfumes fresh like the skin of infants,
Sweet like oboes, green like prairies

Personification: attaching human attributes to something that is not human.

The project ate up all my time.
The gates opened their arms.

Idiom: combinations of words or phrases that have non-literal meanings.

Dodge a bullet
Foaming at the mouth
Keep tabs on someone/something
Kick the bucket

Portuguese: *Macacos me mordam!*
(monkeys bite me) 'to be intrigued or surprised'
French: *faire d'une pierre deux coups*
(to hit twice with a stone) 'to kill two birds with one stone'
German: *Er hat ins Gras gebissen.*
(he has bitten into the grass.) 'he died'

Semantic relationships among sentences

Semantics is much more than the study of word meaning; it is also the study of sentence meaning. One example of sentence meaning that we've already discussed is *ambiguity*; **structural** or **syntactic ambiguity** arises when a sentence has more than one syntactic structure, as shown in Chapter 5. Syntactic ambiguity is therefore a phenomenon in which both syntax and semantics play a role.

We have also briefly discussed the meaning relationships among sentences such as the following:

Spot is a dog.
Dogs are canines.
Spot is a canine.

This relationship, in which one sentence includes the meaning of another (or, put slightly differently, the truth of one sentence ensures the truth of another), is called **entailment**. Here, the fact that Spot is a dog ensures that Spot is also a canine (being a dog entails being canine).

Paraphrases are sentences that are synonymous, or have the same meaning.

> Spot chased the squirrel.
> The squirrel was chased by Spot.
> It was Spot who chased the squirrel.
> It was the squirrel who Spot chased.

Even though different in word order, these sentences have the same meaning: Spot chased the squirrel (and not the other way around). Here's another example:

> My sister has two children.
> My sister is a parent.

These two sentences are paraphrases because *having children* and *being a parent* have the same entailments.

But consider the following two sentences:

> Booth assassinated Lincoln.
> Booth killed Lincoln.

These two sentences might appear to be paraphrases; the meanings of each include that Lincoln died and that Booth killed him. But *assassinate* and *kill* have subtly different entailments; *assassinate* entails 'kill,' but also 'for political purposes,' an entailment that the verb *kill* lacks. These two sentences are therefore not true paraphrases; they do not share all the same entailments.

How sound and structure influence meaning

Semantics overlaps in interesting ways with other components of grammar, and the study of semantics often includes ways in which syntax, morphology, and phonetics and phonology influence meaning. Consider, for example, how we use intonation to convey meaning.

> I thought I told you that LEE bought a new car.
> I thought I told you that Lee bought a new CAR.
> I thought I TOLD you that Lee bought a new car.

Recall from Chapter 3 on sound the discussion of how we also use intonational patterns (that vary from language to language) to change the meaning of an utterance; consider the different meanings of the sentence *You're wearing that?* Produced with rising intonation, this statement can be interpreted as an innocent question or as a (possibly insulting) critique.

Syntax also interacts with semantics in a number of interesting ways, offering a number of directions for research. Consider, for example, the following pairs of sentences.

> My sister is a surgeon.
> *My lamp is a surgeon.
>
> The dog bit the mail carrier.
> *The dog bit sincerity.

Though both sentences in each pair are syntactically grammatical, the second sentence in each pair is semantically anomalous (or nonsensical, just like the sentence *Colorless green ideas sleep furiously*, which we discussed earlier in the book). In the first pair, the anomaly stems from the fact that the verb + adjective combination *be pregnant* must occur with an animate, female subject. In the second pair, the verb *bite* must occur with an animate subject and a concrete, rather than abstract object. In technical terms, different verbs and adjectives, or *predicates*, require subjects and objects, or *arguments*, that meet certain semantic criteria or **selectional restrictions**.

The next set of sentences illustrates yet another way that syntax and semantics overlap.

*She put the car.
She put the car in the garage.

The first sentence is ungrammatical because the verb *put* has only an object, *the car*, following it. The verb *put*, however, requires not just an object, but a location for that object, which is expressed in the second sentence by the prepositional phrase *in the garage*. Not just any prepositional phrase will do here; if we replace the prepositional phrase that expresses location with a prepositional phrase that expresses time, the sentence is ungrammatical.

*She put the car on Tuesday.

The syntactic requirements of the verb *put*, namely that it be followed by both an object and a prepositional phrase, are not enough; *put* must occur with a prepositional phrase with a particular meaning, or **thematic role**, in this case location.

Thematic roles (a partial list)

- Agent: initiator of some action
- Theme: entity that is affected by an action
- Source: entity from which something moves
- Goal: entity towards which something moves
- Location: the place in which something is situated
- Instrument: entity used to initiate some action

The students walked from *the classroom* to *the cafeteria*.
Agent　　　　　　　　　　Source　　　　　Goal

Jordan threw *the ball* to *Taylor*.
Agent　　　Theme　　Goal

When we explore thematic roles in more depth we discover some very interesting puzzles and patterns.

The thief broke the lock with a screwdriver.
A screwdriver broke the lock.
The lock broke.

We typically learn in school that the subject of a sentence is 'the doer of the action,' but notice that the subject of the verb *break* in these sentences is not necessarily acting on its own volition as the agent of the action. While *the thief* might be an agent, *a screwdriver* is an instrument, and *the lock* is a theme. And what about this sentence?

The thief broke her leg.

This can mean that the thief broke someone else's leg, but also that she (the thief) broke her own leg, possibly on purpose but also possibly not (as we typically use the phrase *X broke X's leg*). What thematic roles does *break* assign to *the thief* and *her leg* here?

As we might expect, languages express thematic roles in different ways, and different languages might have different inventories of thematic roles. Consider the following data from Warlpiri (Carnie, 2013). AUX—auxiliary verb, NON.PAST—present tense

Lungkarda ka ngulya-**ngka** nguna-mi.
bluetongue AUX burrow-A lie-NON.PAST
'The bluetongue skink is lying in the burrow.'

Karli ka pirli-**ngirli** wanti-mi
boomerang AUX stone-C fall-NON.PAST
'The boomerang is falling from the stone.'

What do the suffixes *-ngka* and *-ngirli* (glossed as A and C) mean? In the first sentence, *-ngka* marks location (the burrow), and in the second *-ngirli* marks 'the stone' as the source, the place from which the boomerang is falling.

We have offered here only a brief look at the ways in which the study of semantics interacts with the study of other areas of grammar. We now turn to yet another way to study meaning in language, how we use language in different contexts for different communicative goals.

How context shapes meaning: pragmatics

In the examples of meaning in language that we've considered so far, we have not needed to rely on context to understand the meanings of words and sentences. Entailments, contradictions, and paraphrases, for example, can be construed without considering when, how, and with what intention a particular sentence is uttered or used. This is how semantics differs from **pragmatics**, the study of how context influences meaning. The study of pragmatics encompasses a wide range of different areas, including rules of conversation, politeness, speech acts (what constitutes a threat, a promise, an assertion, etc.), and more.

To illustrate how pragmatics differs from semantics, consider the following sentence:

She booked a vacation to Hawaii yesterday.

Semantically, the meaning of this sentence, in isolation, is simply a proposition about booking a vacation to a particular location. But how does the meaning change when we add context?

Speaker A: Did Margaret get some time off?
Speaker B: She booked a vacation to Hawaii yesterday.

Speaker B's utterance, in this context, suggests, without directly stating, that Margaret did indeed get time off, because otherwise it would be very strange to say she had booked a vacation. So in a sense it is an answer, though an indirect one, to Speaker A's question. This interchange illustrates **conversational implicature**, meaning (here, a positive answer to Speaker A's question) that depends on context. This also illustrates how a great deal of meaning in language is neither explicit nor literal, but depends on a speaker's intention and the hearer's interpretation.

Maxims of conversation

We all participate in conversations on a daily basis, and sometimes they go well and sometimes they don't, and we sometimes—but not always—know why. We generally attempt to avoid miscommunication, which suggests that we generally attempt to follow certain conversational rules or principles to say what we mean and be understood. We can also break, or *flout*, these rules sometimes on purpose, to derive a particular result.

Philosopher Paul Grice proposed the following **maxims of conversation**, which continue to be considered a fairly accurate description of the shared rules that speakers use in interactions (Grice, 1975, 1989).

Maxim of Quantity

- Make your contribution to the conversation as informative as necessary
- Do not make your contribution to the conversation more informative than necessary

Speaker A: Did you eat all the pizza in the refrigerator?
Speaker B: I ate the pizza in the refrigerator and I ate the pad thai.

(B's implicature is *yes* – B provides too much information, but enough for A to assume there is no pizza left.)

Maxim of Quality

- Do not say what you believe to be false
- Do not say that for which you lack adequate evidence

Speaker A: Are you ready for dinner?
Speaker B: I'm starving!

(Here, B flouts the Maxim of Quality, but in so doing, implies, *yes*)

Maxim of Relation

- Say only things that are relevant

Speaker A: Can I borrow your car?
Speaker B: The keys are on the table.

(The location of the keys is only relevant if the answer is yes, so B is implying *yes.*)

Maxim of Manner

- Avoid obscurity of expression
- Avoid ambiguity
- Be brief (avoid unnecessary wordiness)
- Be orderly

Speaker A: What's the matter?
Speaker B: I had a fight with my cousin and unfriended her on Facebook.

(B not only provides a clear answer but adds orderly detail of time – the unfriending as a result of the fight.)

Grice's maxims go together with his **cooperative principle**, which assumes that the participants in a conversation will make a "conversational contribution such as is required, at the stage at which it occurs, by the accepted purpose or direction of the talk exchange" (Grice, 1989, p. 26). Basically, this means that in conversation we don't lie, nor do we assume our conversation partners lie. We assume that the conversation is sincere, and that the information expressed is relevant.

Conversations can break down when we violate the maxims. In the following exchange, the Maxim of Quantity is violated. Speaker A's question is not answered because B does not supply enough information.

Speaker A: Where are the keys to the car?
Speaker B: They were right here a minute ago!

Sometimes, we violate the maxims on purpose, to convey a particular meaning. In the following exchange, Speaker B clearly wants to be left alone, and by violating the Maxim of Quantity makes that point very clear.

Speaker A: What are you reading?
Speaker B: A book.

Presupposition

Yet another relationship among sentences is **presupposition**, where we infer, or make specific kinds of logical assumptions.

> Have you stopped washing your car every night?
> I regret that I didn't get you a birthday present.
> I would love to go to Hawaii again.

Each of these sentences includes an implicit assumption (based on a number of factors, including sentence structure, choice of verbs such as *regret*, and adverbs such as *again*):

> You wash your car every night (or at least you used to).
> I didn't get you a birthday present.
> I have gone to Hawaii before.

Presuppositions fall under conversational meaning, or pragmatics, because such sentences only make sense in context if the presupposition is mutually understood by both the speaker and the addressee. Consider this exchange:

Speaker A: I'm sorry I missed your call! I was on the other line with Sherlock Holmes.
Speaker B: WHAT?

Speaker B's surprise is legitimate here, because Speaker A has not already explained that Sherlock Holmes is her nickname for her father, who, in her opinion, asks too many questions about her personal life. Without this context, there is no presupposition that makes the utterance make sense to Speaker B.

We might think of a presupposition as a kind of entailment: The sentence *I regret that I didn't get you a birthday present* appears to entail the proposition that I did not get you a birthday present. But entailment and presupposition can actually be shown to be different. If we negate a sentence with a presupposition, the presupposition remains:

I regret that I didn't get you a birthday present.
I don't regret that I didn't get you a birthday present.

But if we negate a sentence with a particular entailment, the entailment is lost:

Lee has children. (Lee is a parent)
Lee doesn't have children. (Lee is not a parent)

Politeness

Politeness practices of course vary widely across cultures, but one basic principle of politeness seems to be **face**, or the public image one seeks to project (Brown & Levinson, 1987). Linguistic politeness practices appear to be governed by **positive face** (an individual's desire to seem worthy and gain approval) and **negative face** (an individual's desire to be autonomous). When we use **positive politeness** we generally want to avoid offense by being nice, and we don't want to seem openly critical. We may use humor or endearments or other devices to create common ground and solidarity with the addressee. When we use **negative politeness** we try to avoid offending someone by showing deference; we minimize the imposition on the addressee.

In this exchange, Speaker B uses positive politeness, creating common ground with the addressee, Speaker A.

Speaker A: I'm so sorry I'm late!
Speaker B: No problem! I'm the one who is never on time!

And here's an example of negative politeness, where Speaker A tries to minimize the imposition on Speaker B:

Speaker A: I know it's asking a lot, but could you look over my term paper?
Speaker B: I don't have office hours right now but yes, I will.

Politeness is a rich area of study in pragmatics, as practices vary across cultures, intersecting in interesting ways with age, gender, social status, occupation, and many other variables.

Speech acts

Another well-studied topic that falls under pragmatics is how we use language in context to apologize, threaten, order, promise, assert, question, and so on. Different **sentence types** express different **speech acts**:

> **Assertion:** You kiss your fish.
> **Interrogative:** Have you stopped kissing your fish?
> **Imperative:** Stop kissing your fish!

But depending on the context, we can assert, question, and command without using the corresponding sentence type. Below, Speaker B responds with an utterance in imperative form:

Speaker A: I just got us two tickets to the championship game!
Speaker B: Shut up!

Speaker B's utterance could be a command (*Don't tell me this because I don't want to hear it!*) or a positive excited response, something like *That's great and I'm thrilled!* The meaning depends on the context.

Different speech acts have different **felicity conditions**, or conditions under which they can be interpreted accurately. For example, the utterance *I promise you that I will be home for your birthday* is a promise only if the speaker has the means to get home, and if they are sincere in wanting to get home for the celebration. Uttered by someone serving a life sentence in prison, this utterance is not a sincere promise. And consider apologies—when is an apology sincere and when is it not and why? Felicity conditions offer insights.

Consider this exchange:

Speaker A: Your behavior has been despicable!
Speaker B: I'm sorry if anyone was offended by my behavior.

Is Speaker B really apologizing here? They are shifting the responsibility to those who are offended, but are not taking direct responsibility for their actions. Compare the above non-apology to this utterance:

Speaker B: I'm a jerk. I should not have behaved that way and I'm sorry I hurt anyone.

This is a real apology; Speaker B acknowledges wrongdoing, and takes full responsibility for it.

Why study meaning?

In this chapter we've discussed some of the different ways that linguists pursue the study of meaning. We've discussed some of the principles and rules that govern how we interpret the meanings of words and sentences (semantics). We have also discussed some of the ways in which we interpret the meanings of sentences and words in context (pragmatics).

When you study semantics you learn about linguistic meaning, meanings that we derive from words and sentences themselves.

- You can recognize the different meaning relationships among words (synonymy, antonymy, polysemy, ambiguity).
- You can recognize figurative language (metaphor, metonymy, synesthesia, personification, idiom).
- You can identify the different semantic relationships among sentences (entailment, paraphrase).
- You gain insights into the semantics of sentences and how syntax and semantics interact (selectional restrictions, thematic roles).

When you study pragmatics, or meaning in context, you learn about how we create meaning through language.

- You learn about how we create meaning in conversations through conversational implicature, maxims of conversation, and the cooperative principle.
- You learn about how meaning is shaped by politeness practices.
- You learn about how we use different speech acts to create meaning, and how those speech acts are governed by felicity conditions.

The study of meaning has many different applications. Linguists may be involved in advertising and branding, forensic linguistics (analyzing legal language), or they may study how meanings of words shift and change over time, and how new meanings come into the language. What we learn about speech acts can be applied not only in our everyday conversational practices with family and friends but also in the courtroom (what constitutes a threat, or hate speech?), in the workplace (what kinds of speech acts constitute sexual harassment?), the study of literature (speech acts in poetry, drama, and prose), politics (how does context shape political discourse?), and in many other areas. The study of pragmatics also provides us with a window into different cultural practices and how they are expressed in language. Politeness practices differ in Japanese and English, for example, and how one apologizes differs in Korean and English (see Hatfield & Hahn, 2011). Linguists who study Hmong immigrant communities in Wisconsin, have shown how pragmatic differences among Hmong youth, in contact with Anglo-American pragmatics, and older generations who lack such contact, can lead to miscommunication and a shift from Hmong to English among Hmong youth (Burt & Ratliff, 2011).

References

Brown, P., & Levinson, S. (1987). *Politeness: Some universals in language usage*. Cambridge, England: Cambridge University Press.

Burt, S., & Ratliff, M. (2011). *The Hmong language in Wisconsin*. Lewiston, NY: Edwin Mellen Press.

Carnie, A. (2013). *Syntax: A generative introduction*. Hoboken, NJ: Wiley-Blackwell.

Grice, P. (1975). Logic and conversation. In P. Cole & J.L. Morgan (Eds.), *Syntax and semantics volume 3: Speech acts* (pp. 41–58). New York, NY: Academic.

Grice, P. (1989). *Studies in the way of words*. Cambridge, MA: Harvard University Press.

Hatfield, H., & Hahn, J-W. (2011). What Korean apologies require of politeness theory. *Journal of Pragmatics*, *43*, 1303–1317.

Lakoff, G., & Johnson, M. (1980). *Metaphors we live by*. Chicago, IL: University of Chicago Press.

7
Studying language change
Historical linguistics

We briefly explored in Chapter 2 how language changes over time, which is easy to see when we compare Old English, Middle English, and Present Day English. We also introduced the idea that language change is happening right now, as word meanings, pronunciations, and even our syntax changes (slowly but surely). Think about how your own speech may be different from your parents' or grandparents' (I know my own grandmother would never have said *yeah right*, nor would she have *blogged* or even owned a *computer*.) We take up the study of **language variation**, or language change in progress, in more detail in the following chapter; here, we will provide a little more in-depth discussion of **historical** or **diachronic linguistics**, the study of language change over time.

The study of language in the eighteenth century

The study of historical linguistics as we know it today became particularly prominent after 1786, when Sir William Jones gave a lecture at the Royal Asiatic Society, suggesting that the Germanic languages and the Romance languages descended from a common ancestor (or, more specifically, that Sanskrit, Greek, and Latin had a common parent language, and that other Celtic and Indic languages might share that ancestor as well). Prior to this period, these individual languages were certainly well studied, but the focus was on individual languages, not on how they might be related to each other. Work on these relationships among languages, or **language families**, became prominent during the nineteenth century, and marked a shift in the methods that scholars used to study language. Researchers took a more scientific approach, comparing sets of data from different languages and formulating and testing hypotheses based on those data. Specifically, during this time scholars developed the **comparative method**, which we discuss in more detail below. Jones' and others' research lead to proposing that a number of languages of Europe and India can be traced to a common ancestor, a **proto language** called **Proto Indo-European**. Since Jones' speech, research comparing languages to discover their relationships to each other has continued, and many other language families have been proposed. *Ethnologue*, a compendium of the world's languages, lists 152 different language families, some with members as few as two (Yukian) and others with as many as 1539 (Niger-Congo)!

The comparative method and language family trees

By systematically comparing words and sounds in different languages, scholars can determine whether languages are related to each other. Using comparative language data they can reconstruct the common ancestor language of those related languages. Studying the relationships among languages has long been a focus of linguistic science, and here we provide you with a mini-example of how a linguist might use the comparative method to study the relationships among languages.

Consider the words *hand* and *three* from four different Germanic languages (you can refer to the International Phonetic Alphabet in Chapter 3 to understand the pronunciation of each word):

English	German	Dutch	Swedish	
[hænd]	[hant]	[hant]	[hand]	'hand'
[θri]	[dray]	[dri]	[tre]	'three'

Words that are systematically similar across languages are called **cognates**. Cognates exhibit **regular sound correspondences**, or systematic similarities in pronunciation. It's fairly easy to see that the words for *hand* are cognates in the four languages represented here. Notice how different these words are from other words for *hand* in the other languages below. These do not seem to be cognates of the words under consideration here (and in fact, these languages belong to different language families).

'hand' – Korean – *son*   Swahili – *mkono*   Inupiat – *argak*

Now let's consider the words for *three*. Why are these cognates, when they begin with different consonants? We can use the comparative method to explain this.

The word for *three* in English begins with the interdental fricative [θ], but in German and Dutch with [d] and in Swedish with [t]. But if we examine more data (using the scientific method), we find that these languages vary systematically in exactly this way. In English, for example, the words *thunder* and *thumb*, like *three*, also begin with interdental fricatives. But in German and Dutch the same words begin with [d] and in Swedish with [t]:

English	German	Dutch	Swedish	
[θʌndər]	[dɔnɐ]	[dɔndər]	[tuːdøn]	'thunder'
[θʌm]	[daʊmən]	[dœym]	[təme]	'thumb'

By using the comparative method we discover a regular sound correspondence: words native to English that begin with [θ] will have cognates in German and Dutch that begin with [d] and in Swedish with [t]. We find many such regular sound correspondences among these languages, which suggests that they are members of the same language family, in this case, the Germanic language family. (And as you might expect, we do not find these same correspondences in Korean, nor in Swahili, nor in Inupiat, although they exhibit regular sound correspondences with languages in their own families.) A proposed Germanic language family is given below. (There

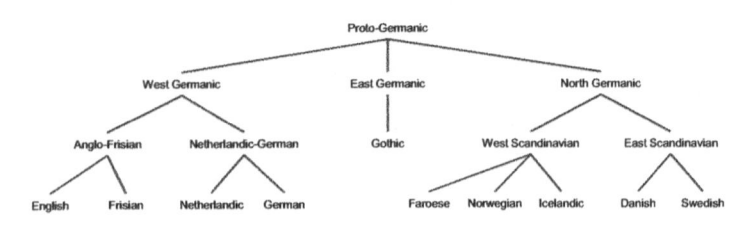

Figure 7.1 Germanic language family

is interesting debate over whether English descends from West Germanic languages or North Germanic languages, including Old Norse. See Emonds & Faarlund, 2014.)

We apply the same method to determine whether other languages might fall into the Germanic language family, or into different families. The comparative method can also be used to determine whether different language families are related to each other, which would suggest they descended from a common parent or ancestor language.

We saw above that we can hypothesize that English, German, Swedish, and Dutch belong to the same language family (Germanic), because of their regular sound correspondences. We come to the same conclusion when we consider data from Latin, French, Spanish, and Portuguese. You can see these languages appear to be related to each other, based on regular sound correspondences.

Latin	French	Spanish	Portuguese	
manus	main	mano	mão	'hand'
tribus	trois	tres	três	'three'

And in fact, Latin, French, Spanish, and Portuguese are members of the same language family, the Romance or Italic family (French, Spanish, and Portuguese, along with Italian and Catalan and Romanian, all descended from Latin).

Proto-Indo-European

We can also show, through regular sound correspondences, that the Germanic language family and the Romance language family are not only related to each other, but to other language families as well. The following table illustrates how we can find regular sound correspondences among members of different languages families (in this case members of the Germanic, Romance, Hellenic, and Indic language families). As you can see in this table, Sanskrit, Greek, and Latin all have words for 'father' that begin with [p], and in Gothic and English, these words begin with [f], for example.

Scholars propose, based on these and other regular sound correspondences, that the Germanic, Indic, Romance, and Hellenic language families descended from a common parent or 'proto' language, called Proto-Indo-European (PIE). We call the language a proto language because it is **reconstructed**; it is no longer spoken and there are no written records. By using the comparative method scholars have determined that there are around ten different language families that descend from Proto-Indo-European, and that there are an estimated 445 Indo-European languages spoken in the world today.

Understanding how languages change over time also allows us to learn a great deal about the people who spoke languages that may now be extinct. For example, linguists have determined that a group of people, who likely lived somewhere in Central Europe around 7000 years ago, spoke Proto-Indo-European. We have no written record of their existence, but we do have a lot of evidence

Table 7.1 Proto-Indo-European word roots

Sanskrit	Greek	Latin	Gothic	English	PIE Root	Meaning
pita	pater	pater	fadar	father	*pater-	father
padam	poda	pedem	fotu	foot	*ped-	foot
bhratar	phrater	frater	brothor	brother	*bhrater-	brother
bharami	phero	fero	baira	bear	*bher-	carry
sanah	henee	senex	sinista	senile	*sen-	old

PIE = Proto-Indo-European; * = possible protoform

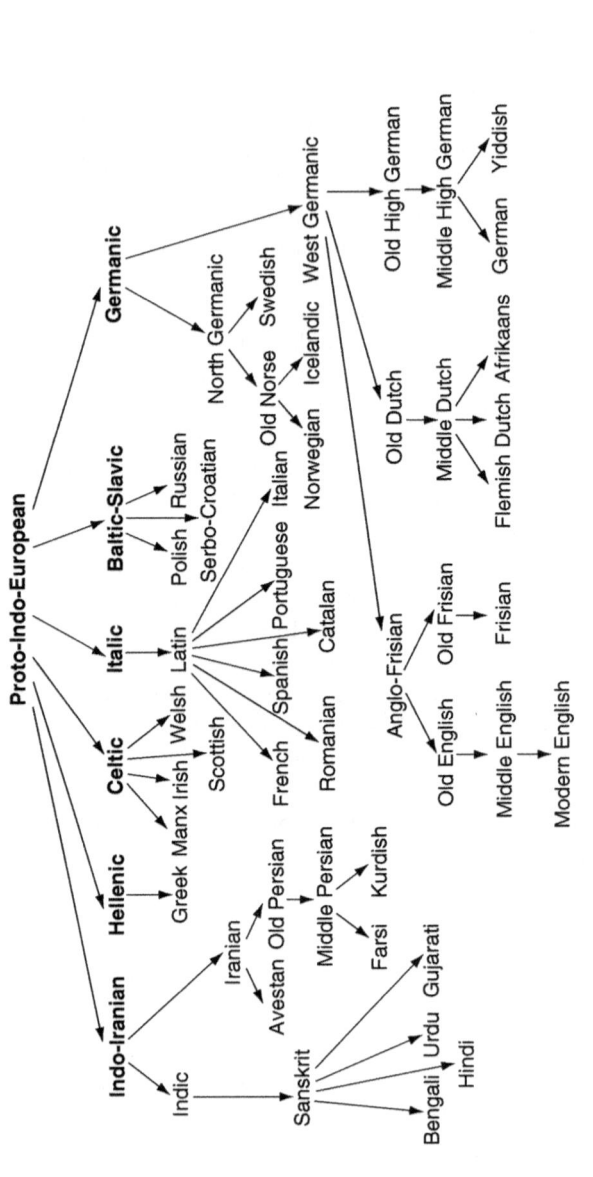

Figure 7.2 Proto-Indo European language family
Image courtesy of Russell Hugo

from the many descendant languages, which has helped scholars establish that Proto-Indo-European was originally spoken in what is now Eastern Europe, likely somewhere north of the Black Sea. By studying the reconstructed vocabulary of Proto-Indo-European, scholars find no words for the sea, but other words for animals and plants of the region, different from the words for animals and plants in languages spoken near the Mediterranean or in Asia. We also can be reasonably certain that the speakers of Proto-Indo-European counted, had the wheel, and believed in multiple gods.

Other language families

As we mentioned above, according to *Ethnologue*, there are 152 language families that have been discovered so far in the world today. Here is just a selection of those 152 families, with the number of languages in each family in parentheses (adapted from Gordon, 2005). Keep in mind that there are estimated to be about 7000 languages in the world.

> "Studying linguistics has helped me to really understand the importance of language in the world and languages around the world."

In North America alone, north of the Mexican border, there are about 300 indigenous languages; the majority of those are grouped

Table 7.2 Sample language families of the world

Afro-Asiatic (376)	Mongolic (13)	Siouan-Catawban (14)
Arauan (5)	Nilo-Saharan (207)	South-Central Papuan (22)
Chinookan (2)	North Caucasian (34)	Tarascan (2)
Chukotko-Kamchatkan (5)	Otomanguean (177)	Trans-New Guinea (482)
Dravidian (86)	Panoan (25)	Uto-Aztecan (61)
Eskimo-Aleut (11)	Quechuan (44)	West Papuan (23)
Hmong-Mien (38)	Sepik (55)	Yanomaman (5)
Kartvelian (5)	Sign Language (142)	Yeniseian (2)
Maipurean (56)	Sino-Tibetan (455)	Zaparoan (5)

into 29 language families, and the remaining are either language isolates, with no known related languages, or remain unclassified. The following list of languages and language groups is a compilation of Campbell (1997), Goddard (1996), and Mithun (1999). The majority of these American languages are no longer acquired as first languages by children. The numbers in parentheses indicate the language varieties within that family that are considered to be distinct languages.

Adai	Iroquoian (11)	Solano
Algic (30)	Kalapuyan (3)	Takelma
Alsea (2)	Karankawa	Tanoan (7)
Atakapa	Karuk	Timucua
Beothuk	Keresan (2)	Tonkawa
Caddoan (5)	Kutenai	Tsimshianic (2)
Cayuse	Maiduan (4)	Tunica
Chimakuan (2)	Muskogean (9)	Utian (15)
Chimariko	Na-Dené (39)	Uto-Aztecan (33)
Chinookan (3)	Natchez	Wakashan (7)
Chitimacha	Nuu-chah-nulth	Wappo
Chumashan (6)	Palaihnihan (2)	Washo
Coahuilteco	Plateau Penutian (4)	Wintuan (4)
Comecrudan (3)	Pomoan (7)	Yana
Coosan (2)	Salinan	Yokutsan (3)
Cotoname	Salishan (23)	Yuchi
Eskimo-Aleut (7)	Shastan (4)	Yuki
Esselen	Siouan (19)	Yuman–Cochimí (11)
Haida	Siuslaw	Zuni

Types of language change

There are, as you can imagine, many ways to study how language changes over time, and research on language families is only one possible area of investigation. Linguists might study *why* languages change: the historical events that lead to change (migration, colonization, wars, famine, disease, contact with other languages, etc.). This is the study of **external change**, or forces external to the language itself. Linguists might also study **internal change**, the syntactic, morphological, phonological and semantic changes that happen over time. Linguists are also interested in discovering what kinds of changes do occur in a language, what changes don't occur, and why not. We give some examples from the study of the history of English below.

Morphological change

How does word structure change over time? We often see this in inflectional morphology; Old English, for example, had many different ways to form plural nouns, but in Present Day English the most common way is to simply add -*s*. As we have discussed in Chapters 4 and 5, this means that Old English was a **synthetic** language; it had a much richer inflectional system than we have today, with inflected nouns, adjectives, and verbs, and even adverbs. Old English nouns, for example, were inflected for gender (masculine, feminine, or neuter), four cases (nominative, accusative, genitive, dative), and number (singular, plural). (Nouns in Modern German are also inflected for these features.) We illustrate here with the noun *scip*, 'ship.'

Nominative singular neuter   *scip*   Genitive singular neuter   *scipes*
Nominative plural neuter   *scipu*   Genitive plural neuter   *scipa*

There were also many different classes of verbs which showed inflection through vowel changes, and some still exist today *(sing/ sang/sung, drink/drank/drunk)*; these are called *strong* verbs.

singan   'to sing'
sang   'sang'
(g)esungen   '(has) sung'

Old English also had many *weak* verbs, verbs that were inflected through affixation (in this case, a suffix), with no vowel change, just as we have today: *walk/walk/walked, play/play/played.*

fremman	'to do'
fremeþ	'he/she/it does'
fremmende	'doing'
fremed	'(have) done'

Though Present Day English still has strong verbs, new verbs that come into the language are weak: *googled/faxed/texted*. Present Day English today is far more **analytic** than Old English, and relies on word order, rather than inflectional morphology, to express grammatical relationships.

New words are also added to languages over time. Compounding was common in Old English, and some examples include *sunbēam* 'sunbeam,' *hēahsynn* 'high sin, crime,' and *ongēanhwyrf* 'backturn, return.' Old English also used affixation to create new words: *brōðor* meant 'brother,' and *gebrōðor* meant 'a member of a community, a monk' (Millward, 1996).

During the Middle English period a number of new words were borrowed into the language, primarily from Norman French after the Norman Invasion of 1066, but also from Scandinavian languages. Norman French borrowings account in part for the vast number of synonyms in English today (*cow/beef, hen/poultry, deer/venison*). Other vocabulary include words for medicine: *medicine, surgeon, disease, remedy*; words for education: *study, science, reason, university*; words for law: *judge, jury, appeal, evidence*; and words for fashion: *fashion, dress, garment, jewel*. Scandinavian borrowings include *awe, birth, droop, firth, glitter, mistake, rugged,* and *skate*.

Phonological change (sound change)

How do pronunciations and other phonological aspects of language (stress, intonation, tones, etc.) change over time and in what ways? Old English, for example, had the sound [v] only between vowels; <f> would be pronounced [v] in *heofan* 'heaven,' for example. After contact with French after the Norman Invasion of 1066, however, English speakers adopted (over time) the sound [v], because many words in French have this sound not only between vowels but at the beginning of words (*vertu* 'virtue,' *vraiment* 'truly,' and *valeur* 'value'). In Old English the sound [r] was trilled, and [g] and [k] sounds at the beginning of the words *gnæt* 'gnat' and *cneow*' 'knee,' were pronounced. English also underwent The Great Vowel Shift sometime between Chaucer's time and Shakespeare's, which dramatically changed vowel pronunciations. This is why if you hear Middle English, the vowels sound very different from our modern pronunciations. For Chaucer, *name* would be pronounced [namə] (rhymes with *llama*), and *clean* would be pronounced [klɛːnə] (rhymes with 'Jenna').

Semantic change

It is fairly easy to see how word meanings change over time, and they change in different ways. A word's meaning can **broaden**, or become more general: *dogge* in Old English used to denote a specific breed of dog, but now means any domestic canine. *Hound*, on the other hand, has gone in the other direction and **narrowed**; it once referred to any dog, and now refers to a specific breed or type. (In German, the word *hund* still means 'dog,' because the changes that happened in Old English did not also happen in German.) *Awful* used to mean 'worthy of awe.' The meaning of this word has not just changed but undergone **pejoration**: it has become more pejorative, or negative, in meaning. Other examples of pejoration include *notorious*, which used to mean 'publicly known,' and *hussy*, which used to mean 'housewife.' Word meanings can also undergo **amelioration**; their meanings become more positive. *Pretty* originally meant 'cunning, wily,' and *nice* meant 'careless, clumsy.' And some changes in word meaning seem arbitrary; *bead* comes from Old English *gebed*, 'prayer' (rosary beads help Catholics count their prayers) but without studying language change, we would probably not make that connection!

Syntactic change

As mentioned above, Old English was more synthetic than Present Day English (PDE), and word order was more flexible. Main clauses were typically SVO, but subordinate clauses were SOV.

S(ubject)	V(erb)	O(bject)
and mæsse-prēost	*āsinge*	*fēower mæssan*

and (the) mass priest (should) sing four masses

Subordinate clause:

S	O	V
for ðan	*Æmær hī*	*becyrde*

because Elmer them betrayed

You can also see in these examples how one word can encode grammatical information that requires two words in PDE, as we would expect in a synthetic language; for example, *mæsse-prēost* requires no separate 'the,' and *āsinge* requires no separate modal, 'should.' How did English come to be strictly SVO in both main and subordinate clauses? That is the kind of question that linguists who study language change might investigate, and in fact, the shift in word order is usually ascribed to the gradual loss of inflectional morphology in English, which led to the language becoming more analytic, and reliant on SVO word order.

Syntactic change can involve not only changes in basic word order (from SOV to SVO, for example, as some have argued has been the case in English) but also changes in other syntactic phenomena, such as how sentences are negated, how questions are formed, how the pronoun system has changed, among many other things. For example, multiple **negation** was common in Old English, and **wh-questions** were formed in a different way as well. Note the absence of *do* in both the negative sentence and in the question (note also that in Old English, question words began with *hw-* rather than *wh-*), taken from Millward (1996):

Hē cwæθ θæt nān man ne būde be norðan him.
He said that no man not lived to (the) north (of) him.
He said that no man did not live to the north of him

Hwilce fixas gefēhst ðu?
Which fishes catch you? Which fish do you catch?

Middle English also had multiple negation, and auxiliary *do* was just beginning to show up in *wh*-questions and in negative sentences:

He nevere yet no vileynye ne sayde
He never yet no villainy not said

Fader, why do ye wepe?
Father, why do you weep?

By the time we get to Early Modern English (late fifteenth century), we can see that English question formation and negation are still in flux. By this time, negative *not* occurs after an auxiliary verb as in PDE, but also at the end of the clause, unlike in the English of today. And *do* appears in questions but not consistently. (Examples from Millward, 1996).

I do not doubt you.
I doubt it not.

Why do you look on me?
Why look you so upon me?

There are many other such examples of syntactic change, and as you can see here, change is gradual, and often both the changed and unchanged forms exist side by side until one becomes adopted fully into the language.

Why languages change

There are many theories about how and why languages change, and here we will briefly outline a few different factors that contribute to change.

Natural processes of language change

Not all of language change is driven entirely by external events; languages also change internally for a number of different linguistic reasons. Think about how your pronunciation changes when you speak casually versus when you speak formally. You may, for example, use contractions such as *gonna*, *don't*, and *supposta* in casual speech, but *going to*, *do not*, and *supposed to* in a job interview. Over time, phonological processes of natural language, such as contraction (which can involve both phonological deletion and assimilation), can give rise to forms that become fixed in the language. In Old English the verb 'ask' was *acsian*, which led to the pronunciation *aks*, which eventually, due to metathesis, became *ask* for many speakers, but not all. Similarly, word meanings change in natural ways, one of which is *backformation*, the process by which we create a new word by removing parts of a larger word. For example, the word *bulldozer* came into English before the verb *bulldoze*, and from *upholstery* came the backformation *upholster*.

Language acquisition

We've seen how the grammar of a language can change over time. This means that the speakers of a language must at some point adopt changes in the lexicon or in other components of the grammar of their language. This suggests that during language acquisition, children might actually transform the grammar of the language, based on input from those around them, who are beginning to adopt certain changes. Recall, too, that children acquire language by teasing out the grammatical rules of the language around them, but they are exposed only to fragments of that language; so what, exactly, must they be exposed to in order to adopt a particular change? This is an interesting question and a topic of study in historical linguistics (see Lightfoot 2006, among others).

Language contact

As we mentioned earlier, migration, colonization, trade, etc. bring languages into contact, which results in language change. Pidgins may crop up among speakers of different languages, and those may eventually develop into creoles. Some speakers may become fully bilingual as a result of contact, but others may use the other language in certain contexts. Language contact often gives rise to borrowing, of words, phrases, grammatical structures, etc.

Social identity

Earlier in the book we discussed how two groups of African American women, the 'church ladies' and the 'porch sitters,' used features of African American English to construct two different social identities. Young people use slang for this purpose (to differentiate themselves from adults in their social groups), and we also use specialized vocabulary or jargon when we talk to those in our particular profession, sport, or hobby. We use language to create our gender identities, and/or to identify with a particular social group in school. Different social identities lead to language differentiation and change.

Why study language change?

When we study language change, we gain a deeper understanding of the dynamic nature of language, and how and why language (inevitably) changes over time. Key findings include:

- Language changes over time as a result of both external and internal factors.
- Through the comparative method and regular sound changes, we can determine family relationships among languages.
- Areas of study include morphological change, syntactic change, semantic change, and sound change.

Historical linguistics also sheds light on other subjects. When we study language change we often study older literature, early writing and spelling systems and connections between them, how languages become endangered and sometimes die or are revitalized, and we also learn a great deal about cultural practices, religious beliefs, and other aspects of human behavior that might otherwise remain buried forever.

We also can also trace back in history the origins of contemporary language attitudes and prejudices. In the United States, many people consider language change to be evidence that English is somehow deteriorating. You have probably heard people say things like 'texting is ruining the language,' or 'swearing denigrates language,' and other similar pronouncements. Some feel that prescriptive rules, which first emerged in England in the seventeenth century, should be strictly adhered to in order to 'maintain' a language in its purest or best form, but as we can easily see by studying language change, change is not only inevitable, but contributes to the dynamic, rich, and creative nature of the language.

> "When people see how language is always changing, they are less likely to think that language is changing for the worse. Like, texting language demonstrates the ways that texters are actually really savvy about their language use and subtle meaning distinctions. I think that's cool, and I think it shows how when people pause to study language—even a little bit—they realize how amazing it is, and how complex it is, and how you need to stop putting people down for the many ways we all use language."

These attitudes about the vagaries of change are still with us today; Steven Pinker devotes a chapter in his book *The Language Instinct* to those he calls 'the language mavens,' self-proclaimed keepers of language who rail against what they see as language decline reflected in usages such as *I could care less* rather than *I couldn't care less*, or in verbs that derive from nouns (*to caveat, to dialogue, to impact*) (Pinker, 1994). We might find such investment in language rules silly, but such attitudes can also be discriminatory, supporting the view that some language varieties have more social prestige than others. The study of language change therefore overlaps in important ways with the study of language variation and socially constructed attitudes about speakers.

References

Campbell, L. (1997). *American Indian languages: The historical linguistics of Native America.* Oxford, UK: Oxford University Press.

Emonds, J.E., & Faarlund, J.T. (2014). English: *The language of the Vikings.* Olomouc, Czech Republic: Palacky University Press.

Gordon, R. (Ed.). (2005). *Ethnologue: Languages of the world* (15th ed.). Dallas, Texas: SIL International. Online version: www.ethnologue.com/. Used by permission of SIL International.

Goddard, I. (1996) (Ed.). *Handbook of North American Indians. Volume 17: Languages.* Washington: Smithsonian Institute.

Lightfoot, D. (2006). *How New Languages Emerge.* Cambridge: Cambridge University Press.

Millward, C.M. (1996). *A biography of the English language* (Vol. 1). New York, NY: Harcourt Brace College Publishers.

Mithun, M. (1999). *The languages of Native North America.* Cambridge, UK: Cambridge University Press.

Pinker, S. (1994). *The language instinct.* New York, NY: Penguin.

8
Studying language variation
Sociolinguistics

Given the enormous social role of language, it is not surprising that much research in linguistics focuses on the role of language in society. Linguists study how language variation correlates with geography or region, and/or they may study how language varies based on social factors, such as ethnicity, race, gender, age, socioeconomic class, and so on. Sociolinguists typically study language **synchronically**, or at a particular moment, rather than over historical periods, **diachronically**. Sociolinguists who study how geography and settlement patterns influence language variation might develop maps of the different language varieties in a particular region or area.

The work that linguists do informs a great many aspects of our daily lives. We notice people's accents and may be able to guess where they spent their formative years. We can usually determine if someone is a native speaker of English or learned English later in life. We like to talk about the different words speakers use—is it a *grocery store* or a *supermarket*? A *sofa* or a *couch*? A *bathroom* or a *washroom*? Do we stand *in line* or *on line* for concert tickets? Do you do something *by accident* or *on accident*? Is it a *mountain lion* or *cougar*? Some variations are points of interest and maybe invite a chuckle. Others, however, are much more stigmatized— the use of *ain't*, verb forms such as *I seen her*, or *We done ate*. Understanding why some variations seem quaint or interesting, while others evoke disdain is critical to understanding the role of language in society, and how language variation and our attitudes toward it play a role in the education system and in the larger society—in teaching a standardized form of the language, in language policy decisions such as laws about English as an official language or bilingual education, or in discussions about non-sexist and non-binary languages, including gender-neutral pronouns.

Language variation and region

We tend to associate dialects with regions; when someone speaks, you may be able to determine that they grew up in the southern United States or in New England or in New York City. You may have a more difficult time discerning the differences in the speech of someone from Colorado and someone from Oregon. And if you are a speaker of American English, you will notice differences in the speech of those from the UK or from Australia. So many of our speech differences correlate with place—and not, of course, because there is something in the water or the very earth the speakers walk on. There are a greater number of dialect distinctions along the east coast of the United States, reflecting still, even several hundred years later, the speech characteristics of the English speakers who colonized those regions. The first permanent settlements of English speakers in the New World were Jamestown, Virginia, in the south in 1607 and Plymouth, Massachusetts, in the north in 1620. We know they were settled by people from England. It is impossible, however, to trace the origins of most of these settlers, for there are no records of where they came from in England, only the port from which the ship sailed (London, in most cases). Many people came in search of religious freedom—the Puritans in New England, the Catholics in Maryland, and the Quakers in Pennsylvania. Others were fleeing economic disaster, and most did not have a lot of education. Though we can say that they spoke what we now call Early Modern English, they did not all speak the same dialect; the British English of the time was (and still is) made up of many regional and social varieties.

Sociolinguists study language variation and the factors that affect it, but when they do so, they might be studying phonetics, phonology, morphology, syntax, or semantics of the language variety; the study of phonology, for example, and sociolinguistics are not mutually exclusive but are very much intertwined. When we study how pronunciation might correlate with sociological factors like income or gender, that is both phonology and sociolinguistics. When we study the continuum of language varieties of a creole from the **basilect** to the **acrolect** (a less prestigious variety and a higher prestige variety) and how these correlate with prestige, among other factors, that is the intersection of grammar and sociolinguistics. It's important to understand such intersections, and that the study of variation very much depends on a solid grounding in the core components of linguistics: phonetics, phonology, morphology, syntax, semantics, and pragmatics.

Dialectology and lexical variation

Early work on dialects and language variation focused on word differences. Who says *pail* and who says *bucket*? Who says *dragonfly* and who says *darning needle*? Early dialectology focused largely on lexical differences, and although such distinctions are waning, they still exist. Consider variations like the following:

cart – buggy
knapsack – backpack
torch – flashlight
vacuum – hoover (originally an eponym, a brand name)
icebox – refrigerator
lorry – truck

These early dialectal investigations, which also included not just words, but also pronunciation and grammatical differences, led to maps that identified boundaries between dialects, such as the one in Figure 8.1, which attempts to recognize the major geographical dialects within the United States today:

It's not the case, of course, that dialects change drastically when one crosses one of the dialect boundaries, and there are many more distinctions that could be made—everyone in the Lower South, for

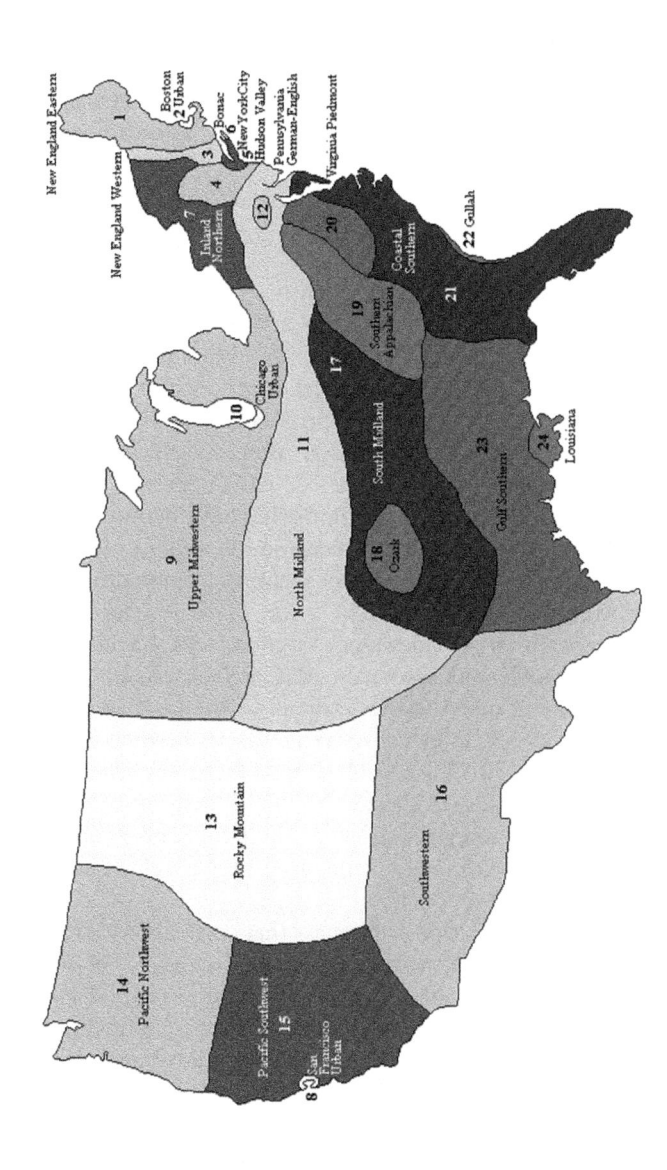

Figure 8.1 Dialect regions of the United States
Copyright 2000 by Robert Delancy

example, does not speak the same way. But these dialect regions attempt to capture some of the similarities and differences that distinguish speakers from certain regions.

Similar language/dialect boundaries exist for all language varieties. Languages do not exist that do not have variation among the speakers or signers of each language.

Phonological variation

The linguistic effects of different British settlement groups that landed up and down the east coast can still be heard in American dialects today. One of those features is the pronunciation of the <r>s after vowels, called **post-vocalic [r]**, mentioned in Chapter 2. While everyone who speaks English pronounces [r] word-initially, as in *red*, some dialects have no [r] after vowels and before consonants, pronouncing *park* more like 'pahk'. Several '*r*-less' or **non-rhotic** dialects of English exist along the coastal United States, in eastern New England and in the deep South, and are attributed to settlement of these areas by *r*-less speakers from southeastern England. Well-known examples of *r*-less dialect areas include Boston, Massachusetts; Tidewater, Virginia; and Birmingham, Alabama. Tidewater was also part of the Southern plantation agricultural system, and *r*-lessness spread to the English eventually spoken by slaves, influencing what was to become African American English. Not all coastal areas of the eastern United States are *r*-less, however; speakers of '*r*-ful' dialects of British English also settled along the coast, as did *r*-ful Scots-Irish from Northern Ireland, who greatly influenced the speech of upland Virginia colonists.

Some other pronunciation differences that correlate with region are the pronunciation of words like *cot* and *caught*. For many speakers in parts of the midwest and west, these words and others are pronounced the same. For other speakers, they remain distinct. This sound variation/change is known as the **low back merger**, since these sounds produced in the mid and lower back part of the mouth, /a/ and /ɔ/, have merged into a single sound. Refer again to the vowel chart from Chapter 3, repeated in Figure 8.2.

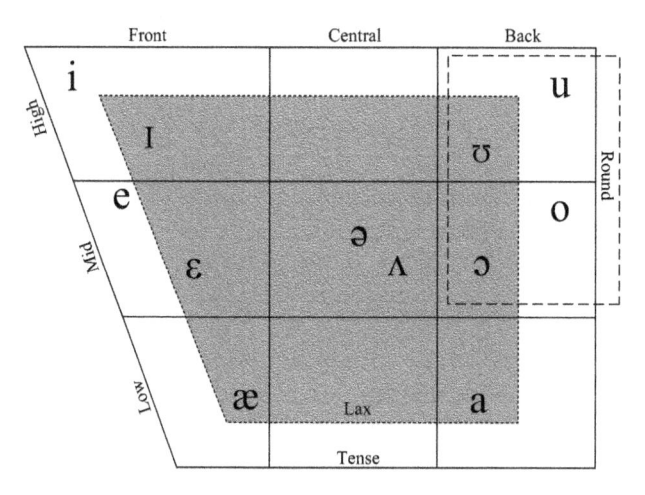

Figure 8.2 English vowels

Another sound variation that correlates with region is the pronunciation of words like *pin* and *pen* and *tin* and *ten* with the same vowel. For many speakers in the southern United States, such words are homophones (*pin/pen* are pronounced as /pɪn/ and *tin/ten* as /tɪn/), while for others, they have distinct vowels, /pɪn/ and /pɛn/ and /tɪn/ and /tɛn/. This vowel merger, which occurs only before nasal consonants, is also beginning to occur in parts of the west, and so is no longer restricted to the southern region.

Factors affecting sound variation

But variation in pronunciation doesn't just correlate with where you're from. William Labov, in a now famous (1966) study, examined how the presence of [r] correlates with speakers' perceptions of social class. We use [r] here to refer to any phonetic variant of [r].

In New York City, the absence of [r] after a vowel is stigmatized (so the [r]s would not occur in words such as *car*, *hear*, *cardboard*) and those speakers who have [r] in those positions, on the other hand, have more social prestige. In Labov's study, researchers elicited the phrase *fourth floor* from salespeople in three department stores: Saks 5th Avenue (high prestige), Macy's (mid-prestige), and S. Klein (low prestige). Salespeople in Saks pronounced [r] 62 percent of the time; in Macy's, 51 percent; and in S. Klein, 21 percent. Labov's study demonstrated that the salespeople adjusted their speech style (unconsciously) depending on perceptions of prestige.

Or consider the differences in the ways Americans generally perceive the pronunciation of [r] after vowels by British speakers compared to American speakers. For one group—British English—the dropping of [r] is a prestige marker; for the other group, it's generally not.

Other linguists study language variation much more locally; Penelope Eckert, for example, has studied the speech of students in a California high school, in particular the vocabulary (use of *like* for example) and vowel pronunciations of what is popularly referred to as 'Valley Girl' speech.

Eckert studied how variables such as gender, age, and social status influence how high school girls talk, and more specifically how these speakers' pronunciations reflect a shift in vowel sounds. The Northern California Vowel Shift indicates that younger speakers' vowels are shifting in patterned ways (Eckert, 2008 and website: https://web.stanford.edu/~eckert/).

Eckert's work shows that a word like *think* is pronounced more like 'theenk.' *Did* sounds more like the vowel we generally expect in *dead, friend* is 'frand,' *brook* is 'bruck,' and *move* becomes almost the bisyllabic 'mi-oov.' Whether these vowel shifts will spread more widely throughout the West, resulting in a language change, is not yet known. Also, there is ongoing investigation of the similarities and differences between the California Vowel Shift and the similar Canadian Vowel Shift.

William Labov has been studying the variation in vowel pronunciation among urban speakers in a group of northern cities in the United States for decades, known as the Northern Cities Vowel Shift (Labov, Ash, & Boberg, 2006). Both Eckert's and Labov's work describe vowel shifts in progress right now, rather than studying vowel shifts as historical phenomena like the Great

Vowel Shift we discussed in Chapter 7. But one day, students will likely study these vowel shifts as historical changes that have already taken place!

Eckert and others have also studied features of language, such as 'creaky voice' or 'vocal fry,' and 'upspeak,' features which are typically associated with women's speech. Their work has shown, however, that these features show up in men's speech as well, and that the often negative attitudes towards these features are likely based on attitudes about gender, rather than on actual linguistic facts.

Morphological variation

All aspects of language can vary across dialects. We have seen lexical differences and pronunciation differences. We'll examine here some morphological and syntactic variations too. Consider the following sentences, each of which has two possible forms for the past tense verb. Though you might find one form more natural than another, neither is particularly stigmatized.

> I dreamed/dreamt about you last night.
> The frog leaped/leapt from the lilypad.
> He burned/burnt the toast.

For the most part, the -*t* forms are decreasing and speakers have been gradually adding more verbs into the -*ed* category. In other cases, however, we have taken a regular -*ed* past tense form and created a new form, modeled on a pattern with vowel change rather than suffix. For example, consider the following:

> I sneaked/snuck into the hallway.
> The girls dived/dove into the pool.
> They lighted/lit the candles.

In these examples, the -*ed* form is the older form, and the vowel change forms (*snuck*, *dove*, *lit*) are the more recent innovations. Though some of the verb forms in these different patterns may be considered less standard, in many cases, the variation has led to language change, with the majority of speakers accepting the new variation, illustrating that language change and language variation exist on a continuum, and that we say that the language has changed when the majority of language users have adopted a particular form. Such examples illustrate how some patterns that we might stigmatize as less standard language variations are not; evaluations of variations are based on social attitudes about speakers themselves, not on some deficiency in the language.

Syntactic variation

Let's examine a particular syntactic variation that results in the presence or absence of a prefix *a-*. This prefix had its origins in an Old English prefix and still remains in some varieties of English spoken on the Outer Banks of North Carolina and in the Appalachian Mountain region. Certain words that end in *-ing* can take an *a-*, pronounced as 'uh,' in front of the word, as in 'She went *a*-fishing.' But not every *-ing* word can have an *a*-prefix; there are patterns or rules that determine when the *a*-prefix can and cannot be used for speakers of these dialects. Those rules depend on the part of speech of the word the prefix attaches to. Consider, for example, sentences such as the following from Reaser and Wolfram (2007), which all work with the *a*-prefix.

> She was a-building a house.
> He went a-hunting.
> He kept a-running to the store.
> The children are a-charming the snake.

While when the *-ing* word is functioning as a noun or an adjective rather than a verb, the prefix cannot attach:

> *A-building is hard work.
> *The children are a-charming.

Most English speakers, even if they do not speak a language variety that makes use of this prefix, can make judgments about the grammaticality of such examples, and are therefore uncovering knowledge that the prefix is sensitive to syntactic categories (only attaching to verbs). This *a*-prefixing grammatical process is typical of Appalachian dialects (and has its roots in much older forms of English coming from the British Isles), but is stigmatized by many other English speakers. It is stigmatized, however, not because of anything about the linguistic patterns themselves but because of attitudes towards the speakers.

Language attitudes and linguistic discrimination

We make all kinds of assumptions about each other based on the way we dress, the kind of car we drive, where we live, and how we talk. The way we talk, our dialect, is intertwined with our identity. It remains somewhat acceptable in our society to criticize people's speech—their accents, their vocabulary choice, their syntax. We can find numerous examples of people making judgments about others' speech, and this discrimination is most obvious with two of the most stigmatized American dialects: Southern dialects and African American dialects (there are numerous varieties of each). The stereotype of Southerners as uneducated, naive, and racist continues to play out in the media, in books, and in schools. It remains quite prevalent even when recognized as unfair and untrue.

This kind of linguistic discrimination is not easy to fix because it is connected to so many complex social issues. However, an important first step, at least, is to recognize where our attitudes about language variation and language change come from and then to contextualize them within our current culture.

> "Studying linguistics has helped me to appreciate all sorts of different linguistic processes. Instead of hearing someone say something that varies from my dialect and thinking, 'That sounds ugly,' I get excited! I analyze these differences now instead of judging them."

We all have biases about language and assume stereotypes about people based on their language, whether we realize it or not. The following are examples of assumptions about language that some of our students have collected:

> "And I can say the same thing in an English accent and it's suddenly so much more sinister."
>
> From a conversation with my roommate about how when reading stories out loud, I always read the villain lines in an English accent

> "I hate when people from eastern Washington pronounce Boise with tons of emphasis on the -se. It makes it sound like you're a backwoods hick."
>
> My roommate discussing people from his native Spokane

> "There's a difference between having good grammar and an accent; some people just didn't learn to speak as well as others."
>
> My housemate in a debate over the proper use of 'who' and 'whom'

> "If I had a southern accent I don't know if I could look at myself in the mirror in the mornings."
>
> My friend

> "I'm way more likely to listen to someone who has an Australian or English accent. They just sound better."
>
> A friend

> "Ebonics is a disgrace to the English language."
> Former high school classmate's Facebook status update

> "I am not pronouncing it wrong; I'm just pronouncing it the only way I can."
>
> My mom, whose native language is not English

"Wow Robert Griffin III is very well spoken for being a Southern athlete."
>Someone on my football team last year

"Yeah, my new math teacher pronounces measure as 'MAYsure.' I can't stand it!"
>Talking to my friend about our new schedules

"Spanish class must be easy for you because you are Mexican."
"Actually, English is my first language."
>Two girls having a conversation in the lounge

"I've never even considered the idea that people from the Northwest have an accent just like people from Boston or another place have an accent, or that our way of speaking isn't just normal. It's only normal to us."
>My friends

"I assumed she didn't know English well because she only spoke to her friends in Spanish. I was surprised to have a full on conversation with her in English; she didn't even have a accent."
>My friend

Stereotypes and attitudes about language varieties exist for all languages everywhere. One could find Spaniards from Madrid criticizing the language of Spaniards from Seville; French speakers from Quebec criticizing the French of Parisians or Ghanaians; English speakers from South Africa critiquing the English of Bostonians; and so on. Some of these statements reveal subtle bias, some reveal underlying incorrect assumptions, and some are outright discriminatory. Sociolinguists Preston (1993), Lippi-Green (1997/2012), Cukor-Avila (2000), and others all provide evidence of discrimination that correlates with regional, racial, or ethnic 'accent' or dialect. Such discrimination can lead to differences in the ways children are educated, in how people are treated in the legal system, in acquiring housing, as well as their treatment in daily life.

Consider a pronunciation variation studied by phoneticians called **creaky voice**, also known as laryngealization or **vocal fry**. Creaky voice is a slow tightening and slackening of the cartilage in the larynx, the 'voice box.' In English, laryngealization or lack thereof doesn't ever make a difference in the meaning of a word, but in other languages, including Mazatec, Hausa, Bura, Bruu, and Mpi, it does. The 'same' sounds produced with and without laryngealization in these languages mean different things. English speakers can produce sounds with creaky voice, but doing so doesn't make a difference in meaning. Some English speakers seem to make use of laryngealization, however, and some perhaps more than others. And some of those who don't have much laryngealization—or don't think they do—seem to have disdain for vocal fry. Listening to female radio announcers who seem to have laryngealization, listeners complained it was "grating," "so annoying," "irritating," and even "too much to bear." This phonetic feature, typically associated with young women even though there is no evidence that women do it more than men, can elicit surprisingly strong feelings. Vocal fry has been called—by non-linguists, mind you—an "epidemic" and an "unfortunate affectation." (These quotes are from *This American Life*, Freedom Fries episode). These strong attitudes seem to stem not from the laryngealization itself, but from societal attitudes related to gender, age, and power.

Linguist John Baugh conducted extensive research on such **linguistic profiling** (2003) focusing primarily on linguistic and racial profiling and housing discrimination, and he has worked with the National Fair Housing Alliance (NFHA) to make people aware of the potential for discrimination based on language. Baugh has demonstrated that there is discrimination against those attempting to rent, based purely on someone's voice. Those with African American dialects or Chicanx or Latinx dialects are often told no rentals are available; when someone with a 'white' dialect calls, however, they are told rentals are indeed available.

The racial and linguistic bias present in the George Zimmerman trial in 2013 has been well documented. Zimmerman was the man who shot Trayvon Martin, and a key witness in his trial was Rachel Jeantel, a friend of Martin's. Zimmerman claimed he acted in self-defense, but Jeantel was on the phone with Martin during the altercation with Zimmerman until just before his death, and she claims that Zimmerman was the instigator. Jeantel's testimony was, therefore, key to the case, but Rickford and King (2016) provide much evidence that racial and linguistic prejudice were at the heart of the discrediting of Jeantel and her testimony.

> "When you study linguistics, you will be informed about language myths and ideologies and will have the tools to confront bias and discrimination (intentional or unintentional), which can be met with reasoned data and facts."

Language policy and planning

Sometimes the use of a particular language or dialect is carefully planned, with official governmental policies developed to ensure that the language is spoken and/or taught in schools. Such deliberate efforts to influence the selection and promotion of a community's language use and acquisition are known as language planning. **Language planning and policy** arise out of socio-political situations where, for example, speakers of various languages compete for resources or where a particular linguistic minority is denied access to basic rights. One example is the U.S. Court Interpreters Act of 1978, which provides an interpreter to any victim, witness, or defendant whose native language is not English. Another is the Voting Rights Act of 1975, which provides for bilingual ballots in areas where more than 5 percent of the population speak a language other than English (see Robinson, 1998 for more information).

Other language planning decisions attempt to meet needs by *reducing* linguistic diversity, as in instances where a language is declared a national language in a multilingual country (such as Bahasa Indonesia, 'language of Indonesia') or where a single language or a single variety of a language is declared the standard or official one to promote linguistic unity in a country where divergent dialects or languages exist. For example, although many dialects of Chinese exist, the promotion of a single variety as the national language (Mandarin) can, some argue, contribute to a sense of national unity.

Often times, however, a top-down attempt to establish language policy can divide and exclude. There is no official language in the United States, though many states do have laws making English the official language. Hawaii is the only state that has a language other than English as the official language; Hawaiian is as well. English-only legislation was proposed in 1981 by Senator Hayakawa of California as a constitutional amendment called the English Language Amendment. If approved, it would have banned all uses of languages other than English in federal, state, and local government. However, the measure has never come to a congressional vote. Since then, however, 31 states have adopted English as an official language, though many of these laws are simply symbolic, stating that English is the official language of the state. These various laws and proposed laws regarding making English an official language are quite controversial, sometimes pitting basic rights against linguistic unity.

> "How I grew up played a large role in how I feel about language. My mom is not a native English speaker—her first language is Korean. A lot of my family members on that side were only allowed to speak Japanese for their childhood; they were forced to learn it in school during the Japanese annexation of Korea. Growing up, my family lived in post-Soviet countries where the local languages had been suppressed in favor of Russian. I got to learn Tlingit while I lived in Alaska, where I was shocked to learn that the same thing had happened to Alaska Natives. Without hesitation, the most important thing I have ever learned is how much pain and shame goes into securing the right to speak your own language. Taking that native language away from anybody is an injustice."

Why study language variation?

When we study language variation and sociolinguistics, we gain a deeper understanding of the specific and rule-governed ways in which language varies and the factors that affect it. Key findings include:

- Language varies in systematic ways in all areas of the grammar: phonetics, phonology, morphology, syntax, and semantics.
- Factors affecting and correlating with variation include region, race, ethnicity, class, and age.
- Attitudes towards and opinions about language variation are often socially based.

Public controversies in which linguistic knowledge, and in particular awareness of patterns of discrimination, is critical include the use of Pidgin (Hawaiian Creole English) in schools in Hawaii; determining the best ways to teach children English in school; maintaining the language(s) of the home; and teaching about the potential downsides of Official English laws, which can range from reducing time for bilingualism to severely affecting people's civil rights.

Knowledge of language variation informs so many realms—language biases remain a powerful discriminatory means to wield power and privilege, and a recognition of the way not only that individuals use language and language differences to discriminate, but also how institutions and society writ large do, is a critical component of movement towards a more just and equitable world.

Other ways that those who study language variation might make use of this knowledge working with language and the law as forensic linguists; as dialect coaches for actors; teaching English to speakers of other languages; and in K-12 teaching more generally, where knowledge of how and why language varies is critical.

References

Baugh, J. (2003). Linguistic profiling. In S. Makoni, G. Smitherman, A.F. Ball, & A.K. Spears (Eds.), *Black linguistics: Language, society, and politics in Africa and the Americas* (pp. 155–168). London, England: Routledge.

Cukor-Avila, P. (2000). Revisiting the observer's paradox. *American Speech, 75*(3), 253–254.

Eckert, P. (2008). Variation and the indexical field. *Journal of Sociolinguistics, 12*(4), 453–476.

Labov, W. (1966). *The social stratification of English in New York City*. Washington, DC: Center for Applied Linguistics.

Labov, W., Ash, S., & Boberg, C. (2006). *The atlas of North American English: Phonetics, phonology and sound change. A multimedia reference tool.* Berlin, Germany: Mouton de Gruyter.

Lippi-Green, R. (1997/2012). *English with an accent: Language, ideology and discrimination in the United States.* London, England; New York, NY: Routledge.

Preston, D.R. (1993). The uses of folk linguistics. *International Journal of Applied Linguistics, 3*(2), 181–259.

Reaser, J., & Wolfram, W. (2007). *Voices of North Carolina dialect awareness curriculum.* Retrieved June 2018 from www.ncsu.edu/linguistics/research_dialecteducation.php

Rickford, J., & King, S. (2016). Language and linguistics on trial: Hearing Rachel Jeantel (and other Vernacular speakers) in the courtroom and beyond. *Language, 92*(4), 948–988.

Robinson, D.W. (1998). The cognitive, academic, and attitudinal benefits of early language learning. In M. Met (Ed.), *Critical issues in early second language learning: Building for our children's future* (pp. 37–43). Glenview, IL: Scott Foresman Addison Wesley.

9
Studying language in the brain
Psycholinguistics

As you read about in earlier chapters, a central question of linguistics is how we acquire knowledge of language as children. A great deal of evidence suggests that humans are born with the capacity to acquire language and are equipped with some inherent knowledge of language, making the complex task of acquiring language relatively easy, regardless of intellectual capacity, circumstances, or the language that one is exposed to. Psycholinguistics, or the psychology of language, encompasses a great many aspects of the study of language. Some claim, as Noam Chomsky himself has (1972), that linguistics itself can be considered a branch of psychology since psychology is the study of the mind and behavior, and the study of language is an important component of understanding the human mind and human behavior. Psycholinguistics is typically understood to include the study of the acquisition of language by children (sometimes known as L1 acquisition); the processing of language at all levels (phonological, morphological, syntactic, and at the discourse level); and the storage and access of words in the lexicon. Experimental methodologies common in psychology, such as eye-tracking, reaction time, and neural imaging, are often used to assess various aspects of language production, processing, and storage.

First language acquisition

Child language acquisition provides us with a great deal of evidence for our innate capacity for language. Neuropsychologist Eric

Lenneberg compares the acquisition of language to innate abilities in other species, including eyesight in cats and flight in birds. All such behaviors, he argues, share the following characteristics of biological behavior (Lenneberg, 1967):

- The behavior emerges before it is necessary.
- Its appearance is not the result of conscious decision.
- Its emergence is not triggered by external events (but the surrounding environment must be appropriate for it to develop adequately).
- Direct teaching and intensive practice have relatively little effect on the behavior.
- There is a regular sequence of milestones as the behavior develops, and these can be correlated with age and other aspects of development.
- There is likely to be a critical period for the acquisition of the behavior.

As we've seen above, language acquisition in children emerges with exposure to linguistic input, but not out of necessity or decision. Acquisition proceeds through developmental stages regardless of culture or environment, as long as the child is exposed to language. Teaching, correction, and reinforcement seem to have negligible effects on language acquisition, and although acquisition proceeds in stages, these stages do not seem to be correlated with any other aspects of development. Language acquisition, like flight in birds or eyesight in kittens, is therefore very different from a learned behavior, such as playing the piano or riding a bicycle—or learning a second (or third or fourth) language in school.

Children acquire language regardless of where they live, what language they are exposed to, how much or how little they are spoken to, or what their intellectual abilities are. By studying how children acquire language, the patterns that emerge, the mistakes they make, and the stages they go through, we can learn a great deal about language more generally.

And what sorts of evidence exist for a critical period for language acquisition? Simply put, children appear to be much better than adults at acquiring language. Some have argued that the best time to acquire a first language is from birth to just before puberty. Children exposed to language for the first time after this developmental period are less likely to acquire language fluently or natively. But the concept of a critical period for language acquisition is controversial and hard to test; although there are cases of children deprived of exposure to language during early childhood, such cases are (thankfully) very rare and also complicated by other factors that affect language acquisition. Perhaps the best known case is Genie, a child isolated from language until about age 13. Although Genie was able to learn some language after she was exposed to it, she never developed a full grammatical system (see Curtiss, 1977). There are other cases beyond Genie's that also support the critical period hypothesis; deaf children of hearing parents might not be exposed to linguistic input (sign language) from birth, and Newport (1990) and others have shown that early exposure to sign language is crucial in order to fully acquire the grammar of the language. (See also Newman, Bavelier, Corina, Jezzard, & Neville, 2002). There is much anecdotal evidence as well in support of a critical period for language acquisition. Many of us have experienced sitting in a high school language classroom memorizing vocabulary and learning verb tenses. The relative difficulty of this scenario and the ways in which it is different from the much more natural and effortless process of children acquiring a language is evident. Or let's say a non-English-speaking family moves to the United States; the young children will acquire the grammar of English perfectly and speak with an American accent, while the adults will have a much more difficult time. Their critical period of language acquisition ended around puberty and the brain's ability to acquire language in the same way that children do has closed. Or suppose you're an adult, and you travel to another country and are immersed in the language there. You already speak a native language, so how does the process of becoming proficient in this second language proceed? Does your first language help you learn a second language, or does it hinder that process? How do you keep the grammar of each language, the native one and the second one, straight? If you are learning a second language as an adult, your brain is already mature, so do you go through the same developmental stages learning that language as you do acquiring your native language as a child? These are the kinds of questions that those interested in language acquisition attempt to answer in various ways via scientific investigation.

> "I had so much fun after studying language acquisition realizing what 'language machines' the kids I babysit for are."

Language acquisition rules and strategies

We have seen that knowing a language means knowing (unconsciously) a system of rules, a grammar, which allows us to produce and understand that language. A related question central to the study of linguistics is: how do we come to know this system? How do we come to produce and understand language at such an early age, by age 4–5, without being taught? No parent teaches their child the syntactic, semantic, phonological, or morphological rules of a language, yet children somehow eventually master these rules, and they do so at a relatively early age. Many people might assume that we acquire a first language by being directly taught it, but first language acquisition involves much more than learning and/or memorization. One of linguist Roger Brown's well-known examples of child language acquisition is given below (Brown, 1973):

Child: Want other one spoon, Daddy.
Father: You mean, you want THE OTHER SPOON.
Child: Yes, I want other one spoon, please, Daddy.
Father: Can you say "the other spoon"?
Child: Other...one...spoon.
Father: Say..."other."
Child: Other.
Father: "spoon."
Child: Spoon.
Father: "Other...Spoon."
Child: Other...spoon. Now give me other one spoon?

As you can see from this exchange, correction has little effect; for the child at this stage, 'other one spoon' is completely grammatical and follows the child's own internal rules. Although the child will at a later stage of development produce 'the other spoon' consistent with adult grammar, this will only happen when the child is ready, not because of instruction, correction, or repetition.

Children produce and understand sentences that they've never heard before, and clearly do not learn language by simply memorizing all the possible sentences of that language. Nor can they acquire language by imitation (which would require hearing a sentence before ever being able to produce it—consider a child who yells *I hate you Mommy!* Or says *I finded all the treasure! She runned to the pool*—these sentences are certainly not learned simply by imitation!). Rather, children seem to construct, based on the language that surrounds them, a set of grammatical rules, rudimentary at first, but becoming more and more sophisticated as language develops. For example, English-speaking children typically *overgeneralize* plural *-s* and past tense *-ed*, producing forms such as *foots* and *sheeps*, and *goed* and *buyed*, before they refine those rules, producing *feet* and *sheep* or *went* and *bought*. Children at age two or three do this on their own and seem fairly impervious to intervention. Later on, kids are sensitive to correction and conform to fit into their language communities. Consider situations like being criticized for using *ain't* or changing your pronunciation of a word when hearing how someone else pronounces it: *epitome, apricot, nuclear*. These changes occur due to social pressure. But very young children don't care about that and follow their own rules—which are always systematic.

We mentioned in Chapter 2 the universality of the stages of first language acquisition; children go through the same stages at approximately the same age, regardless of what language they are exposed to, how much or how little they are spoken to, and how 'smart' they are. What accounts for this natural progression of language acquisition in humans, regardless of culture, environment, language structure, or intellectual abilities? Research suggests that the human brain is 'hardwired' in some way to acquire language when exposed to it. Put slightly differently, the young human brain is language ready, making the task of acquisition effortless and unconscious. But how, exactly, do children do this?

A child growing up in an English-speaking household does not have to hear every English sentence in order to master the language; in fact, such an enterprise would be impossible, given the infinite number of possible sentences of English! When you think about it, the kinds of linguistic input we are exposed to as children are rather chaotic and incomplete. Children acquire the grammar of the language around them, language that includes stops and starts, incomplete sentences and phrases, short sentences, long sentences, some complex and some not. Nevertheless, at a very early age children seem to be able to tease out the relevant principles and rules of language that allow them to construct and understand sentences, including sentences they have never heard before. This is what linguists refer to as the logical problem of language acquisition, which poses the question: how do children, faced with fragmented linguistic input—sometimes called *the poverty of the stimulus*—acquire a full linguistic system?

What kids' 'mistakes' tell us

Research and psycholinguistic investigation on first language acquisition explores this question from a variety of different perspectives, revealing many fascinating aspects of this biological behavior. Children seem to not only eventually acquire the grammatical rules of the language they are exposed to, but there is evidence that even some of their so-called mistakes are not random. For example, Crain, Thornton, and Tesan (2007) set up an experiment to invite their young research subjects to produce certain kinds of questions. They observed a two-year-old child producing questions such as the following:

What do you think **what's** in there?
(adult version: What do you think is in there?)

What do you think **what** she said?
(adult version: What do you think she said?)

What is relevant here is the placement of the word *what* (in boldface) in the child's question; in the adult version, this word is absent: *What do you think is in there?* The questions this child produces are not only different from the adult versions, but they could not have been learned through imitation; English-speaking adults never produce questions like this.

What Crain et al. found, however, was that the child's questions conform perfectly to questions in some varieties of German, where *was* ('what') occurs in this position:

Was denkst du was darin   ist?
what thinks you what therein is
'What do you think is in there?'

Was denskt du was sie gesagt hat?
what think   you what she said   has
'What do you think she said?'

This and other acquisition studies provide evidence that humans have an innate capacity to acquire any *possible* language, because we all share the same kind of brain, and thus the same blueprint for language. It is not surprising that during the process of language acquisition a child might produce an utterance that is possible in another language, just not in their own. Over time and without instruction, the child will tease out which rules conform to their native language, and will ultimately produce grammatical utterances in that language.

Studying language acquisition and syntax

Let's examine this example a bit more closely; it's not just that this English-speaking child's language matches German syntax that's of interest here. These kinds of data also offer insight into our theories of grammatical structure. Studying language acquisition offers a way to test our scientific theories about language. Let's consider how such questions are formed in English and how they differ from declarative statements. In the experiment discussed above, a child asks the experimenter about the objects in a box. The non-question statement about this scenario would be something like the following:

> You think the marbles are in there.

But when we form a question in English, the question word about the unknown information—in this case *what* in place of *marbles*—appears at the beginning of the sentence. So the subject of the subordinate clause (*the marbles* in the clause *the marbles are in there*) moves from its original position to the beginning of the sentence:

> You think **what** is in there?

> **What** do you think _____ is in there?

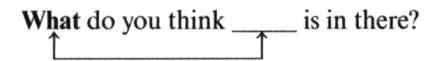

This is known as *wh*-movement, which was mentioned in previous chapters, and is a theory about how we form questions in a variety of languages. The example above of a child producing this example:

> What do you think what's in that box?

offers some support for that theory since the child produces *what* in both the original and moved position and does so not because they are imitating what they've heard, but because they are constructing a theory of language in their own mind. Studying language acquisition, therefore, offers ways of testing theories of grammar and furthering our knowledge of how language works.

Psycholinguistics and Idioma de Señas de Nicaragua

As you might be aware, there is a large and very active Deaf community and culture in the United States. When *Deaf* is capitalized, it is used to refer to those who identify as part of this community and culture. Deaf children of deaf/Deaf parents who use American Sign Language (ASL) are exposed to language at an early age, and acquire sign language in relatively the same stages as hearing children acquire speech. Deaf children can attend schools for the deaf, including Gallaudet University in Washington, DC. The study of sign languages, by linguists, including psycholinguists, has enriched our understanding of many aspects of language.

One such ongoing study is the case of Nicaraguan Sign Language, or Idioma de Señas de Nicaragua (ISN). Before the 1970s, there was no deaf community in Nicaragua; deaf children in hearing communities were isolated from exposure to sign language. During the 1970s and 80s schools for deaf children were created, but the children had no common sign language, only 'home signs' and gestures or 'mímicas' that they had developed to communicate with the hearing community. Teachers attempted to teach the children Spanish, lipreading, and finger-spelling, without much success. Over time, however, the children began to develop their own shared rudimentary linguistic system. Linguist Judy Kegl, an expert on ASL, was asked to help teachers understand what the children were signing, and her research revealed that the older children had developed a rudimentary sign system. The younger children made the system increasingly more grammatically complex. There are now native signers of a full sign language, ISN, and much research is conducted on the language and with the ISN community (Senghas, Kita, & Özyürek, 2004, Morgan & Kegl, 2006, among others).

The case of ISN tells us much about the biological capacity for language. Deaf children created a rudimentary form of the language virtually out of nothing except contact with each other. That the younger children, not the older ones, eventually turned the rudimentary sign language into a full grammatical system provides some evidence for the critical period hypothesis. In the words of Steven Pinker (1994), "We've been able to see how it is that children—not adults—generate language, and we have been able to record it happening in great scientific detail. And it's the only time that we've actually seen a language being created out of thin air." (Kegl, 2009 argues that the development of ISN differs in crucial ways from the genesis of other creole languages, and therefore should not be classified as a creole language.)

The exploration of the ways in which languages of different modalities (signed and spoken) are similar and different in not only their acquisition but also their grammar, including morphology, syntax, and even phonology (which, despite being associated with sound, has components corresponding to phonemic features in signed languages), their processing and production, and the localization in the brain allow for many possibilities for further psycholinguistic research.

Brain lateralization and language functions

An important feature of the nervous system is the fact that the connections between the brain and the body are almost completely contralateral; that is, the right side of the body is controlled by the left hemisphere and the left side of the body is controlled by the right hemisphere. This means too that sensory information from the right side of the body is received by the left hemisphere, while sensory information from the left is received by the right. And in general, the hemispheres don't duplicate each other's functions—each side has its own specific functions. In 1861, Paul Broca, a French physician, observed that damage to the left side of the brain resulted in impaired language ability, while damage to the right side did not. Broca had to wait until his patients died and then he performed autopsies to confirm his ideas. Today's techniques for learning about the brain are much less invasive, and we have many more scientific tools to study the brain, including electroencephalography (EEG), positron emission tomography (PET) scans, and functional magnetic resonance imaging (fMRI). Using these techniques, we can detect and observe charged electrical activity in the brain, and we find that there is much more activity on the left side. In other psycholinguistic experiments, we have learned that there is increased electrical activity in a part of the brain known as the auditory cortex when sound is first perceived. (However, we also find that the term 'auditory' may be a misnomer because experiments show increased electrical activity in the area for those who use sign language in response to flashes of light.)

An individual's early experience and exposure to particular languages' features may help determine brain circuitry. For example, Japanese speakers seem to process single-vowel sounds such as *ooh* and *ahh* in the left hemisphere, as speech sounds, while English speakers perceive these same sounds as emotional utterances, and therefore process them in the right hemisphere. Or native speakers of Thai, which uses tones—variations in the pitch of individual sounds to convey meaning distinctions— tend to perceive tone as linguistic material, while English speakers, for example, filter out the tone and send it off to the right hemisphere.

Much can be learned about the brain too from colossally sectioned, or so-called split-brain, patients. Our two brain hemispheres are connected by the corpus callosum, but to control certain kinds of severe epilepsy, the corpus callosum is severed, preventing the two hemispheres from transmitting information to each other. And when such a patient is, for example, blindfolded and an object is placed in the right hand, the patient can name the object; when, however, the object is put in the left hand, they can't name it (since the left hand transmits information to the right hemisphere, which cannot access the language center of the brain in the left hemisphere).

Another piece of evidence for left hemisphere language dominance comes from dichotic listening tasks, which demonstrate what's called the Right Ear Advantage. Two different linguistic sounds are played simultaneously through headphones to the left and right ears, and listeners are to say what they hear. Subjects give faster and more accurate results to the sounds presented to the right ear since the sounds travel directly to the left hemisphere. For those presented to the left ear, the sound goes to the right hemisphere and then has to travel over to the left hemisphere to be 'languageized,' which results in a slight delay. In the image in Figure 9.1, *ga* would be perceived first, before *ba*.

Although there is evidence that language resides in the left hemisphere, there is also evidence that factors such as literacy,

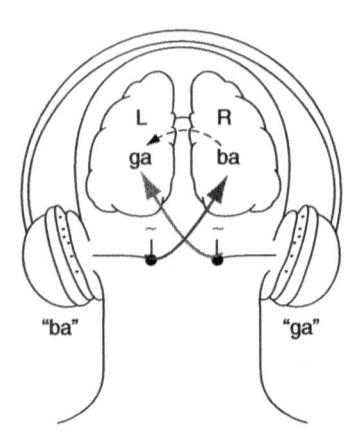

Figure 9.1 The right ear advantage for speech sounds

multilingualism, gender, and others may affect hemisphere dominance, so there is much research still to be done.

Aphasia and localization

We can learn a great deal about language (and the brain in general) by studying people with language impairments. **Aphasia** is a broad term, encompassing many syndromes that impair communication. From studying aphasics, linguists, psychologists, and neurolinguists try to learn not only how to help those with aphasia, but also to discover more about the areas of the brain focused on language, how the nervous system goes about encoding and decoding language, and even whether the components of language—phonology, syntax, semantics, and morphology—have distinct locations in the brain.

Broca's aphasia is associated with trauma to the left hemisphere inferior frontal gyrus, referred to as Broca's area. People with Broca's aphasia have labored speech, with short sentences and long pauses. Karl Wernicke was a German physician who noticed

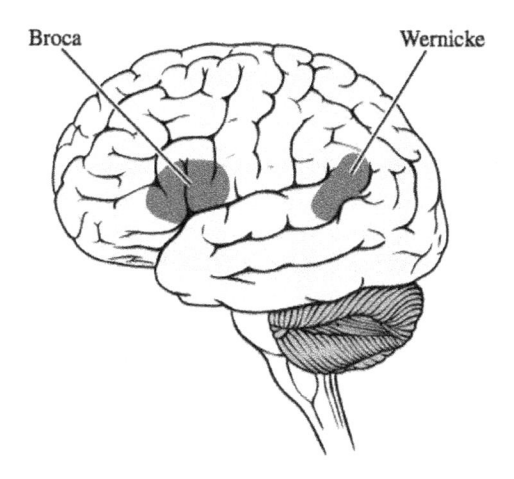

Figure 9.2 Lateral view of the left hemisphere of the brain
Image courtesy of Russell Hugo

that people with damage to a certain area of the brain, the left posterior, superior temporal gyrus, which came to be known as Wernicke's area, had language deficits other than those associated with Broca's aphasia. Because damage to certain areas results in certain kinds of deficits, we might be tempted to conclude that there is a syntax area in the brain or a phonology area. The brain is much more complex than that, but by studying the details of what aphasic patients can and cannot do, we can learn a great deal beyond just language **localization**—where the language centers of the brain reside—but also how they interact. For those who have suffered damage to Broca's area, their spontaneous speech is non-fluent, the rate of speech is very slow, there is much stumbling over words, and they only use major lexical, open class categories—nouns, verbs, adjectives—but not inflectional affixes or closed class/function words. Because of this last fact, some have concluded that Broca's aphasia might be primarily a syntactic deficit. These aphasic patients also seem to have difficulty understanding or producing passive sentences, such as

Bo was seen by Mo.

They typically assume that Bo was the actor or 'agent' doing the seeing, rather than the other way around. And homophones provide additional evidence for the distinction between content words and function words; a Broca's aphasic could recognize and produce words like *bee* and *oar*, but not *be* and *or*, providing additional evidence not only for a distinction between category types (content and function words), but also that Broca's aphasics have difficulty accessing function words. Broca's aphasia is sometimes called 'non-fluent aphasia,' because individuals with this disorder have trouble producing, but not necessarily understanding, language. Wernicke's aphasia, by contrast, is sometimes referred to as 'fluent aphasia,' because individuals with this disorder can produce fluent utterances, but those utterances often don't make sense. Wernicke's aphasics therefore seem to have the ability to produce speech, but not to fully understand it. We can learn a great deal about language in the brain from studying those who have language impairments of one kind or another. And importantly, the language impairments suffered by aphasics are rarely due to any general cognitive or intellectual impairments, nor are they due to loss of sensory or motor control of the nerves or muscles used in speech. Aphasics can produce and hear sounds, and whatever losses they may have involve the production and/or comprehension of language. Those who are hearing impaired and then suffer brain damage show the same kinds of deficits as hearing patients with brain damage. It should be noted, however, that brain damage is rarely going to affect just Broca's area or just Wernicke's area. Isolated damage to the brain resulting in aphasia typically comes from strokes, gunshot wounds, or other traumatic brain injury, so there will likely be damage to other areas as well. Some other aphasic symptoms might include omission of verbs only, or of function words, or of inflectional endings. Some might involve phonological issues, substituting initial phonemes, though the substituted sounds aren't random; they would differ in place or manner of articulation, so, for example, an alveolar stop /t/ might occur in place of the alveolar fricative /s/, so *song* would be *tong*.

Factors affecting language in the brain

More recent research with modern technology has shown that the assertion that language is located (only or primarily) on the left side of the brain might be too general. Other areas seem to also be involved in language use, and Broca's and Wernicke's areas also seem to process more than just language (music, for example). These advances and ongoing investigations deepen our understanding of language as a very complex biological behavior.

Striking evidence for the malleability of children's brains comes from the fact that when children have hemispherectomies—the removal of all or most of the left hemisphere, typically done in order to control severe epilepsy—they can still acquire and maintain language fairly well. The right hemisphere seems able to take over most language abilities if it gets an early enough start. Hemispherectomies in adults result in much more language dysfunction.

Some of the most fascinating research on aphasia comes from bilingual aphasics. Doctors have a difficult time predicting which language will be recovered first or best after brain damage for those who use more than one language. Some regain one language completely, and the other not at all; some regain one language first or better; and some get back both languages at the same rate. There are many ideas about what factors might affect language recovery—the language known best, the last one used before injury, or perhaps the one that is heard most during recovery. Consider the example of a French- and Arabic-speaking nun in Morocco who had a moped accident and became aphasic (Grosjean, 1982). She went through several stages: four days after the accident, she could speak some Arabic, but no French; two weeks later, she could speak French fluently, but by the next day, her French had disappeared completely. After that she remained fluent in Arabic only. Aphasia is more likely to affect a bilingual speaker when there's been right hemisphere damage than a monolingual, suggesting that some of a bilingual speaker's linguistic ability is located in the right hemisphere. This research among other more recent psycholinguistic investigations suggests that the neural basis for language in bilinguals may be different than in monolinguals, and it may also be the case that the languages themselves may reside in different parts of the brain.

Experimental methodologies

Beyond observing and analyzing language acquisition, using brain imaging techniques, or observing and testing those with brain damage, how can we investigate how language is processed in the brain? There are a variety of methods common in psycholinguistic research.

Our understanding of language—both of words and of sentences—seems to happen automatically, without our conscious knowledge. How is it that when a particular sequence of sounds or letters or signs occurs, a particular set of memory traces are triggered in our brains?

Sometimes a computer analogy is useful—we search words in our mental dictionaries much like a computer search occurs. One type of experimentation concerned with how words are stored and composed uses association time—how long it takes a subject to respond to a stimulus, which can then lead to hypotheses about what those different reaction times suggest about the organization of the lexicon. One type of task is called a lexical decision task. At its most basic, a subject is shown a sequence of letters (typically on a computer screen) and asked to decide whether it is a word. So a subject might see *elephant* and respond "yes" and *belephant* and respond "no." Another technique is eye-tracking, which measures eye movement, where the idea is that a subject lingers longer on unfamiliar or more complex words. Of course, there are many variables that could affect access time, and researchers take these into account; two of the most common, and for which there is evidence from other experimentation, is the frequency of the word and whether the word is 'primed.' Across subjects, more frequently occurring words have faster reaction times than less frequent words. And words that have been recently used are more quickly accessed; this is called the repetition effect. But context can also prime words. Lexical decisions are faster for a word like *dog* if the word closely follows a related word like *cat* or *collar*. It suggests that words that are semantically related are 'stored together,' whether that means physically together or with excited neurons or synaptic connections.

Another kind of context effect is when the syntax and semantics of an utterance lead to an expected word. For example, if a subject sees:

She stays up late every night; she's such a night ____

and is then presented with the word OWL or the word BIRD, we predict that they would respond much faster to *owl* than to *bird* due to the context priming effect.

These kinds of experimental techniques and their results suggest that at least one way words are organized in mental dictionaries is by their meaning, or their semantic fields: words that have to do with dogs, people in your family, body parts, etc. Additional evidence for semantic organization comes from slips of the tongue; for example, you mean to say *hot* and you say *cold*; you mean to say *yesterday* and you say *tomorrow*. The slips are never random, but rather indicate how we organize words and concepts.

We also access words based on their phonology, as evidenced by slips of the tongue as well. You mean to say *symphony* and you say *sympathy*; you mean to say *cup* and you say *cut*. So our lexical organization may have what we might think of as multiple cross-indexed filing systems, and some psycholinguists set out to investigate more about those systems of mental organization.

Other experiments try to determine how we negotiate ambiguity. There is some evidence that when words are ambiguous, they take longer to access, suggesting that all meanings of an ambiguous word are accessed. This seems to be the case, even when the context would make it clear which of the meanings is intended. For example, early psycholinguistic research (MacKay, 1966) presented subjects with a partial sentence that contains an ambiguous word, such as the following, where *right* has two meanings:

> After taking the right turn at the intersection...

They take longer to finish the sentence than when there is no ambiguity, as in the following:

> After taking the left turn at the intersection...

Through such investigation, psycholinguists can learn about how language is organized in the brain, how it is processed, and what kinds of factors affect that processing.

Sentence processing

In additional to ambiguous words, psycholinguists also study ambiguous sentences and those that can be difficult to process or to 'parse.' One example of such a sentence is known as a garden path sentence (from the phrase 'lead down the garden path,' suggesting some kind of misleading or trickery), in which a sentence is initially misinterpreted. Some of the classic examples are the following:

> The horse raced past the barn fell.
> The woman returned to her house was happy.
> The florist sent the flowers was pleased.

These are all grammatical sentences, but if they seem ungrammatical or weird or nonsensical to you, it's because you've been 'led down the wrong garden path.' These sentences contain what are called reduced relative clauses. Consider these modifications to the sentences above:

> The horse that was raced past the barn fell.
> The woman who was returned to her house was happy.
> The florist who was sent the flowers was pleased.

Then they become fine, right? And in many cases, we do 'reduce' relative clauses and it doesn't lead to confusion. (*The woman I saw yesterday is a student / The woman that I saw yesterday is a student*) The issue with these is that we construct a syntactic representation in which the first word of the reduced relative clause—above in the *horse* sentence, *raced*—is initially interpreted as part of the main clause. The first tree structure in Figure 9.3 shows the way that we likely construct such sentences initially, based on the typical expected patterns of English syntax. However, upon encountering *was*, such a structure would fail; there is another verb, but our syntax has no structural position for another verb. Thus, the second tree structure in Figure 9.4 offers the 'rebuilt' correct structure that matches the actual meaning.

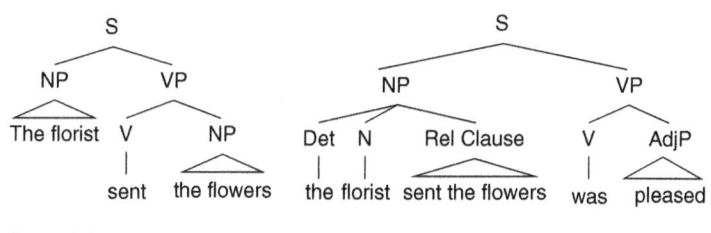

Figure 9.3

Figure 9.4

A method of investigating how sentences are processed is through the use of EEG recordings, called ERPs (Event-Related (Brain) Potentials). Although the precise cognitive processes reflected in these components are unknown, researchers have found that there are different types of responses to different types of 'anomalies.' ERP studies of processing in sentence contexts were initially motivated by the findings of Kutas and Hillyard (1980a, 1980b, 1980c), who found that contextually inappropriate words elicit what is now called the N400 effect, a negative-going brain response that peaks at about 400 milliseconds. And then researchers (Neville, Nicol, Barss, Forster, & Garrett, 1991; Osterhout, 1994; Osterhout & Holcomb, 1992) found a distinct brain response, known as the P600, to syntactic issues.

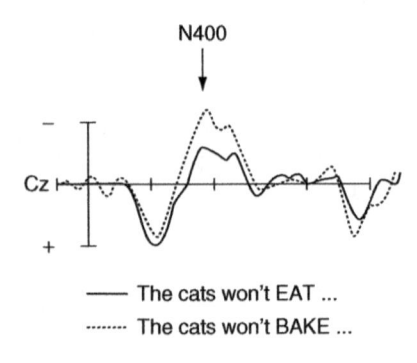

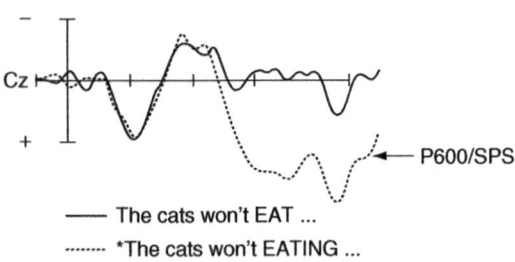

Figure 9.5 Event-related brain potentials illustrating semantic/pragmatic and syntactic anomaly

Such experiments allow researchers to confirm their hypotheses about the different levels of organization of language—that syntax is distinct from semantics, for example—and to then use those differing brain responses to investigate other related topics, such as how bilinguals process language, how these brain waves might differ for different types of syntactic or semantic anomalies, whether a violation is a syntactic or semantic issue, the role of context and pragmatic influences, and more.

Research, using a variety of different methodologies, has shown that language processing can be delayed by perceived mismatches of stereotypical gender information, suggesting that stereotyped gender information may be a part of the mental representation of words, such as *surgeon* or *politician*, which appear to be encoded as male; or *nurse* or *secretary*, which may be encoded as female. It has been widely documented that when language users encounter stereotypically incongruent information (male nurse or female doctor), their processing slows down (Banaji & Hardin, 1996; Kreiner, Sturt, & Garrod, 2008, among others). Thus, psycholinguistic experimentation can provide evidence for some sociological biases, thus enabling examination from various perspectives.

Why study psycholinguistics?

When we study psycholinguistics, we gain a much deeper understanding of how language is acquired by children, how language is processed and produced, and how language is stored in the brain. Key findings include:

- Language acquisition occurs in regular and specific ways, regardless of language.
- Studying the ways in which child language varies from adult language can reveal a great deal about the underlying knowledge we all share.
- Language is lateralized in the brain, with the language center residing in the left hemisphere.
- Experimental methodologies can be used to further understand how language is processed and produced.

Those who have knowledge of psycholinguistics can help people with aphasia; can determine ways in which first language acquisition is similar to and different from acquisition by adults; can explore mental representation, both to help us learn more about what it means to be human and to help us understand distinctions between the mind and the brain and the influence of both internal and external factors on language.

Teachers can make use of many of the insights of psycholinguistics; a clear understanding of the processes involved in first language acquisition and how those differ from second language acquisition is important to working with speakers of other languages. The benefits of bilingualism and how it positively affects brain development is information that can be used to promote the teaching of other languages. Speech language pathologists and clinicians must have knowledge of the features and rate of the acquisition of first and second languages and must be able to distinguish language disorders from language variation or from simple stages of acquisition.

> "Knowing what we know about language acquisition and the importance and benefits of learning languages, I really want to work to use my linguistics background to advocate for more language study in earlier grades. The benefits are numerous and everyone should have the opportunity."

References

Banaji, M., & Hardin, C. (1996). Automatic stereotyping. *Psychological Science*, 7, 136–141.

Brown, R. (1973). *A first language: The early stages.* Cambridge, MA: Harvard University Press.

Chomsky, N. (1972). *Language and mind.* New York, NY: Harcourt, Brace, Jovanovich.

Crain, S., Thornton, R., & Tesan, G. (2007). How children ask questions. [Video]. Retrieved June 2018 from www.youtube.com/watch?v=YuY_Up6rZ_A

Curtiss, S. (1977). *Genie: A psycholinguistic study of a modern day 'wild child'.* New York, NY: Academic Press.

Grosjean, F. (1982). *Life with two languages: An introduction to bilingualism.* Cambridge, MA: Harvard University Press.

Kegl, J. (2009). The case of signed languages in the context of pidgin and creole Studies. In S. Kouwenberg & J. Victor (Eds.), *The handbook of pidgin and creole studies* (pp. 491–511). Hoboken, NJ: Wiley-Blackwell.

Kreiner, H., Sturt, P., & Garrod, S. (2008). Processing definitional and stereotypical gender in reference resolution: Evidence from eye-movements. *Journal of Memory and Language*, 58, 239–261.

Kutas, M., & Hillyard, S.A. (1980a). Event-related brain potentials to semantically inappropriate and surprisingly large words. *Biological Psychology*, 11, 99–116.

Kutas, M., & Hillyard, S.A. (1980b). Reading between the lines: Event-related brain potentials during natural sentence processing. *Brain & Language, 11,* 354–373.

Kutas, M., & Hillyard, S.A. (1980c). Reading senseless sentences: Brain potentials reflect semantic incongruity. *Science, 207,* 203–205.

Lenneberg, E. (1967). *Biological foundations of language.* New York, NY: John Wiley.

MacKay, D.G. (1966) To end ambiguous sentences. *Perception & Psychophysics, 1,* 426–436.

Morgan, G., & Kegl, J. (2006). Nicaraguan Sign Language and theory of mind: The issue of critical periods and abilities. *Journal of Child Psychology and Psychiatry, 47*(8), 811–819.

Neville, H.J., Nicol, J.L., Barss, A., Forster, K.I., & Garrett, M.F. (1991). Syntactically based sentence processing classes: Evidence from event-related brain potentials. *Journal of Cognitive Neuroscience, 3,* 151–165.

Newman, A.J., Bavelier D., Corina, D., Jezzard, P., & Neville, H.J. (2002). A critical period for right hemisphere recruitment in American Sign Language processing. *Nature Neuroscience, 5*(1), 76–80.

Newport, E.L. (1990). Maturational constraints on language learning. *Cognitive Science, 14,* 11–28.

Osterhout, L. (1994). Event-related brain potentials as tools for comprehending language comprehension. In C. Clifton, Jr., L. Frazier, & K. Rayner (Eds.), *Perspectives on sentence processing* (pp. 15–44). Hillsdale, NJ: Erlbaum.

Osterhout, L., & Holcomb, P.J. (1992). Event-related brain potentials elicited by syntactic anomaly. *Journal of Memory & Language, 31,* 785–806.

Pinker, S. (1994). *The language instinct.* New York, NY: Penguin.

Senghas, A., Kita, S., & Özyürek, A. (2004). Children creating core properties of language: Evidence from an emerging sign language in Nicaragua. *Science, 305,* 1779–1782.

After studying linguistics

In addition to the specific approaches to the study of language discussed thus far, the study of language invites overlap with many other academic disciplines in the sciences and social sciences, including biology, psychology, computer science, speech and hearing sciences, anthropology, and sociology. Linguistics courses or courses with a component focused on linguistics are central to a plan of study for students in psychology and cognitive science, anthropology, and speech and hearing sciences, in particular. And in these disciplines, one can even have a title such as linguistic anthropologist, computational linguist, or neurolinguist.

> "I'm so glad I'm studying linguistics! It's a unique major that combines aspects of different social sciences and humanities. It's really helped me to appreciate interdisciplinary perspectives, to be a good humanist, and to think scientifically."

Language can also be studied in the humanities within philosophy, literature, creative writing, communication studies, rhetoric, history, and of course is related to the study of other languages. Linguistics, therefore, is at the core of the study of the sciences and humanities. Other sciences do not necessarily have such an overlap; linguistics is therefore unique in bridging the sciences and humanities.

> "I'm glad I'm studying linguistics because it's the best possible combination of fields—math, cognitive science, formal logic, anthropology, English, sociology, anthropology, psychology—it's got it all! It's impossible to get bored and there's always something to learn."

And the number of students studying linguistics continues to rise. The chart presented in Figure 10.1 from the Linguistic Society of America (LSA, 2017) shows steady growth of undergraduate degrees in linguistics since the mid-1990s.

Such growth is also true for advanced degrees in linguistics, shown in Figure 10.2 for five-year spans beginning in 1966.

So if you are one of those who has studied linguistics, or who is considering studying linguistics, or who has learned something about linguistics via some of the related disciplines and topics, now what? After you've studied linguistics, what can you do with it? A lot. Studying linguistics prepares you for a lot.

In this chapter, we focus on careers that take advantage of your specific skills and knowledge acquired as a student of linguistics. Increasingly, there are more and more jobs and careers in which the knowledge and skills you acquire studying linguistics are applicable and desirable—and known to employers.

Some of the more traditional paths for those who study linguistics include careers in education; speech language pathology; editing, publishing, and journalism; the tech industry; marketing; language documentation and revitalization; forensic linguistics; polyglot jobs, including translator, interpreter, diplomat, or humanitarian aid worker; and a whole lot more.

Careers in education

The routes that lead from linguistics into education are numerous and varied. There is, of course, the direct route to graduate school in linguistics with the result that you become a professor of linguistics, so we'll give that its own section here.

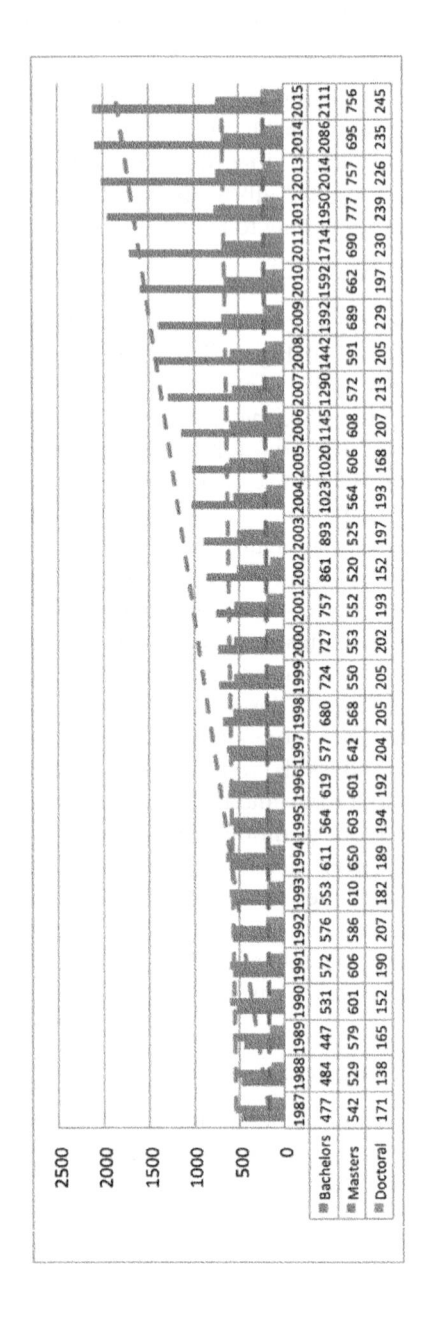

	1987	1988	1989	1990	1991	1992	1993	1994	1995	1996	1997	1998	1999	2000	2001	2002	2003	2004	2005	2006	2007	2008	2009	2010	2011	2012	2013	2014	2015
Bachelors	477	484	447	531	572	576	553	611	564	619	577	680	724	727	757	861	893	1023	1020	1145	1290	1442	1392	1592	1714	1950	2014	2086	2111
Masters	542	529	579	601	606	586	610	650	603	601	642	568	550	553	552	520	525	564	606	608	572	591	689	662	690	777	757	695	756
Doctoral	171	138	165	152	190	207	182	189	194	192	204	205	205	202	193	152	197	193	168	207	213	205	229	197	230	239	226	235	245

Figure 10.1 Trends in the growth of linguistics degrees

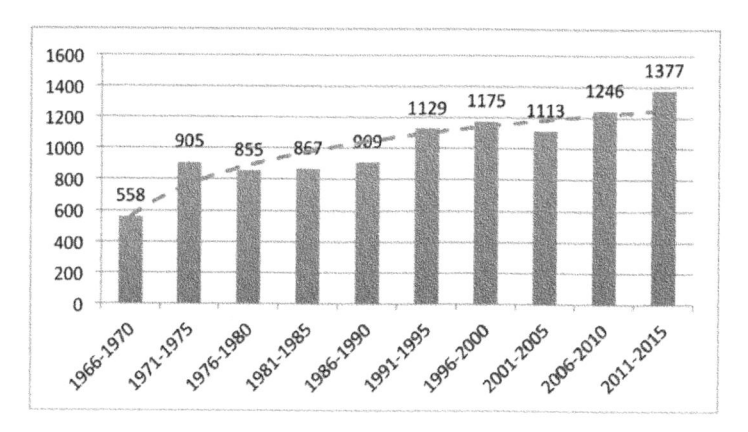

Figure 10.2 Linguistics doctorates awarded across five-year spans 1960–2015

Linguistics professor at a college or university

This route to teaching college students about linguistics nearly always requires a PhD in Linguistics. It used to be that getting a PhD in Linguistics would only prepare you to teach in another institution that offered PhDs in Linguistics. But there are a great many more options these days, and it's useful to know about the various kinds of institutions within higher education you might end up in as a professor of linguistics. Though not all colleges and universities offer an undergraduate major in Linguistics, there are a growing number each year that offer a bachelor's degree in Linguistics. According to the 2017 Annual Report of the Linguistic Society of America, "More students are pursuing and completing degrees in linguistics. In the last decade or so, this has been particularly true for undergraduate degree production" (p. 15).

Research universities

Although conducting your own research and having a solid scholarly agenda is part of any tenure-track or tenured position, there are typically higher expectations at PhD-granting institutions, also known as R1 institutions, for scholarly output. One must publish and stay current in one's field in order to maintain employment. Many schools that offer linguistics at the graduate level also have undergraduate programs, so in most of these, you would teach both the undergraduates and graduate students who are getting their own Masters and/or PhDs in Linguistics.

Undergraduate colleges

If you teach at an undergraduate college, you might end up teaching a wide variety of courses. Your courses also might be less specialized and might be developed to be of interest to a wider range of students (such as 'Language in a Multicultural Society,' 'Linguistics for Non-Majors,' things like that). Research is still an expectation for faculty who teach at undergraduate institutions, though high importance is also placed on teaching.

Community colleges

Research and publication of that research is not as much of an expectation at community colleges (though fewer of them offer Linguistics anyway), nor for adjunct or part-time college instructors. In these jobs the focus is on teaching rather than research; thus, linguistics as a research field is not well represented. Community college jobs can be an important place to focus on teaching and to have access to a wide range of students who might not otherwise have the chance to learn about linguistics.

> "Studying linguistics has helped me to decide where I want to go after graduation—namely grad school, and academia thereafter. I've found an outlet for my love of theory and language!"

Beyond higher education, however, there are many other ways in which linguistics preparation can play out in the world of education, broadly defined. Just a few of these routes are offered in the following sections.

K12 education

If you become a teacher in the K-12 school system, there are many ways that linguistics can come into your classroom, and the benefits of studying linguistics for teachers cannot be underestimated.

Over the last several decades, research in linguistics has led to a deeper understanding of language structure, language variation and change, bilingualism, language learning by children and adults, language disorders and speech errors, and the relation between spoken and written language, among many other topics that are directly related to K-12 education. Linguists have refined their theories of grammar and an increasing number of linguists have been conducting research that applies this new, deeper understanding of language to education. Therefore, there is a critical need for teachers who have a background in linguistics. (See Adger, Snow, & Christian, 2002/2018; Denham & Lobeck, 2005, 2010; Rickford, 1999; Wheeler & Swords, 2004, among others.)

Angela Roh, a high school teacher in Seattle, gives examples of ways in which she brings linguistics into the classroom every day, from "reminding them about informal and formal registers in writing and in speech"; to vocabulary lessons, in which she emphasizes how much students already know about the parts of speech and uses that information to help them understand and use new words; to the use of *they* as a referent to a non-gendered, unspecified person; e.g. *Someone called for you. Oh, really? What did* they *say?* She also ties it into literature:

> When we read Langston Hughes or Mark Twain, for example, I give a lesson on dialects in America and how they are a reflection of region or social group and do not reflect intelligence or lack thereof... The dialect lesson gives them a richer

> appreciation for whatever we are reading and also teaches them a thing or two about judging others... I also have the kids examine their own dialects and try to get them to understand that if they were somewhere else in the US people might think they talked 'weird' too.
>
> (Personal communication)

In American Literature class, she talks about pidgins and creoles when reading slave narratives, about Gullah when reading *Bre'r Rabbit*, and about Native American languages when reading Native literature. (See also Roh, 2010.)

Beth Keyser, a high school teacher from Montana who integrates linguistics into her high school English classes, discusses how she employs an investigative methodology in her classroom, writing:

> One of the major strands in Common Core is problem solving. Completing [language] lessons turns students into scientists of language. They have to discover the rules for themselves based on evidence that *they* look for. Also, students use their own intuitions to understand the rules. This approach is more engaging because every student works on this together in small groups and they collaborate to discover, using evidence, the most appropriate analysis. From my experience, most students do well with this regardless of their reading and writing abilities.
>
> (Personal communication)

Specialized instructors such as reading teachers, resource/special education teachers, and bilingual teachers typically have some background in linguistics. The coursework for teachers in these specialized positions necessarily involves linguistics, and given the changing demographics and increased awareness of linguistics as a field and its applications, more Education programs are requiring linguistics for teachers of all stripes. For example, Western Washington University, where both authors teach, has a degree in which students receive a Bachelor of Arts in Education: Language, Literacy, and Cultural Studies, which emphasizes the importance of increasing "teacher candidates' cultural competency and capacity to teach English language learners." And at the state level, linguistics courses are required for teachers of English. Language study is not only of importance to English Language Arts teachers; it is also being integrated into social studies classrooms. Linguists Jeffrey Reaser and Walt Wolfram have developed language materials for use in eighth grade social studies classrooms in North Carolina; theirs is "the first state-based curriculum on language variation in the country." The goals of this curriculum are:

1. To develop a respect for the systematic patterning of all language varieties
2. To develop an appreciation for the link between historical development and language
3. To develop an awareness and appreciation for the connection between language and culture
4. To gain authentic knowledge about how dialects pattern
5. To develop an awareness and appreciation of other ways of speaking

Another social studies curriculum is in development in Washington State; a collaboration between middle school teacher David Pippin and linguist Kristin Denham incorporates language study into the state-mandated curriculum on Washington state history (Denham & Pippin, 2018). And Christina Higgins in Hawaii has developed materials and a website on Hawaiian Creole English—better known as Pidgin—for use in schools.

> This site provides educators with ideas for teaching about Pidgin and using Pidgin as a resource for learning about history, multiculturalism, the law, and social change in Hawai'i. The site also acts as a central place where ideas about Pidgin can be exchanged.
>
> (Higgins, n.d.)

Also, linguists Maya Honda and Wayne O'Neil have long advocated for using linguistics to introduce scientific methodology.

See, for example, Honda (1994) and the collaborations of Honda, O'Neil, and Pippin.

There are also PhD programs whose focus is on Educational Linguistics, such as the well-known ones at Stanford University and the University of Pennsylvania; faculty and graduate students in these programs work at the intersection of education and language study.

> "I'm currently studying to be an elementary school teacher. But after taking education classes, I still had a lot of lingering questions about how to actually teach the nuts and bolts about language and to promote diversity in my classroom. So I decided to add linguistics as a second major since I realized that all that information would be immensely useful for me in my teaching career. I strongly believe that linguistics strengthens my foundation as a teacher—and it's fascinating! I think that all teachers of all subjects should study linguistics."

Most students don't have the opportunity to study linguistics in high school, but in some places that's beginning to change. There is a national committee working now to introduce an Advanced Placement (AP) Linguistics course across the country, and linguistics is already offered as a high school course by some teachers, including Suzi Loosen in Wisconsin and Ian Connally in Texas. Also, the North American Computational Linguistics Olympiad (NACLO) offers high school students a chance to participate in a problem-solving competition involving linguistic data.

Teaching English to Speakers of Other Languages (TESOL)

TESOL should be recognized separately from K-12 teaching. Many K-12 school districts have some sort of English as a Second Language (ESL) or English Language Learners (ELL) program as part of the K-12 system, and as the number of students who come to school with a home language other than English grows, such programs are increasing as well. Schools have various kinds of ESL, ELL, and bilingual programs, and linguistics students who take college courses in TESOL or TESL (Teaching English as a Second Language) are then prepared to work in many capacities with non-native-speaking adults and children. One route for an ESL/ELL teacher is in K-12 schools, but those with training in linguistics and ESL/ELL also teach at the college level both domestically and internationally. An aspect of this training that attracts many students is that as an ESL teacher, especially one with TESOL certification or a masters in TESOL, can live and work in many places around the world. The ways of doing so are numerous—some work for private companies teaching their employees English, some work in schools, some work for tutoring organizations, some work for the government.

Each country has a variety of programs primarily for native English speakers to teach English in their country, such as the JET program in Japan, the Teaching Assistant Program in France, and many others around the globe. Jennifer MacDonald, an ESL teacher at Dalhousie University in Nova Scotia, Canada, has a BA in linguistics and an MA in TESOL, which is typical of many ESL teachers. Jennifer, who was interviewed by Gretchen McCulloch of *allthingslinguistic*, discusses the importance of linguistic analysis for providing clearer explanations:

> Linguistics gets you used to looking at language and analyzing it. So you can look at a student's text and see that they are making a particular error systematically and figure out what they need to do to correct it. It also makes you better at explaining things about the language, so rather than just saying, 'Oh, that's an exception,' and having your students parrot things, you can really figure out how it works.

Jennifer also simply sings the praises of her career as an ESL teacher:

If you have this interest in language in use, and you have a teaching personality, ESL teaching can be something that's fun and interesting everyday. It's a really great job. Anyone who works in education realizes that just as you're preaching the values of lifelong learning to your students, you're also embodying that too: someone might ask you a question about an obscure verb tense and you need to look it up, and you're constantly figuring out how to better explain things. One of the things I like about teaching is how creative it is.

A lot of students get into linguistics because of their interest in learning languages. TESOL can be one logical outgrowth of that interest.

"I majored in linguistics for a variety of reasons. First, languages have interested me ever since I was young—at age 8 I was already trying to teach myself German and Choctaw. This interest escalated as I studied French, Korean, American Sign Language, and Japanese later on in my life. As I grew older, I found an interest in teaching, but wasn't sure how to combine my passion for languages with teaching until I reached college and discovered the Teaching English to Speakers of Other Languages (TESOL) program. Probably halfway through my TESOL experience, I realized that I wanted to become an even better teacher for my students, especially in the difficult subjects of pronunciation and grammatical structure, so I took linguistics, and I realized that I could use linguistics as a platform to become a better teacher (and a better language learner!). I'm very excited to see what else I can do with linguistics throughout my career!"

Testing agencies

Companies that develop and offer testing, including The College Board (responsible for the SAT) and the Educational Testing

Service (ETS—responsible for the GRE [Graduate Record Exam], TOEFL [Test of English as a Foreign Language], and many other tests) offer employment for those with linguistics backgrounds within this broad field of Education. They hire those with BAs or coursework in Linguistics to those with PhDs in Linguistics or Computational Linguistics. Mika Hoffman completed a PhD in Linguistics in 1991 and has been involved in working with language testing and testing agencies ever since:

> When I finished my PhD in linguistics, ETS hired me to work on the GRE; they sought out philosophy and linguistics graduates, because in their experience those were the people who had the training in precision of language and thought that they needed for high-stakes testing. I soon found that the deep thinking about language that I'd learned by studying linguistics was indeed helpful in crafting clear, unambiguous test items, and I found the work very satisfying, as I tried to make sure that we were aligning the test material with what we were trying to test, and eliminating confounding variables such as hard-to-understand questions. I later moved on to language testing with the Defense Language Institute, which allowed me to use my understanding of how language works to address all kinds of challenges, working with speakers of other languages to figure out the "real" meaning of a phrase in languages I didn't speak. Language testing is a fascinating field, and people with linguistics backgrounds are hugely valuable, even if they don't speak many other languages. I'd advise new linguists to seek out work with language testing companies: there's a lot of really interesting work going on in that field.

Rachel, who completed an internship with ETS, writes:

> Interning with ETS provided me with an opportunity to learn about the test development process from start to finish. At ETS, I built upon my prior experiences in linguistics and teaching, while also gaining new perspective on those experiences.

As part of the ETS team, I created lessons for teachers of ELLs and created numerous test items. The ETS internship provides unique and excellent training in writing and analysis. Throughout my internship, the ETS mentors gave me extensive, personalized feedback, equipping me with the tools necessary to improve my writing and analytical skills and gain a better overall understanding of language assessment.
(www.ets.org/careers/ell_internship/testimonials)

Most importantly, the knowledge and awareness that those with linguistics backgrounds bring to understanding the larger enterprise of standardized testing is critical. For too long, tests have privileged certain language varieties, thereby continuing to perpetuate the myth that intellect and academic success correlate with certain linguistic prestige markers. Charity Hudley and Mallinson (2014) and Reaser, Adger, Wolfram, & Christian, (2017) offer important ways to recognize language patterns and elevate them. Testing agencies need linguists to work with them.

Non-profits

Non-profit organizations such as the Center for Applied Linguistics (CAL) and the Frameworks Institute are at the intersection of education and public policy. At CAL, they "conduct research, develop language assessment and instructional materials, provide professional development and technical assistance services, offer online courses, and disseminate information and resources related to language and culture," according to their website (www.cal.org/what-we-do). And their team works to "conduct original research in the field, and facilitate collaboration nationally and internationally among scholars and other stakeholders." They are also "committed to making significant contributions to the dialogue and debate about language planning and policy with the goal of expanding language choices and widening the context within which language policy decisions are made." Another non-profit, the Frameworks Institute, "designs, conducts and publishes communications research to prepare non-profit organizations to expand their constituency base, to build public will, and to further public understanding of specific social issues." Their purview, therefore, is much larger than language and language issues, but they have several employees with linguistic backgrounds because of the centrality of language to their broader purpose.

Such non-profits may engage in various kinds of language policy and language planning, but work on language policy doesn't occur only within educational non-profits. Those with knowledge of language policy and its effects are important to the efforts of various educational systems at the local, state, and federal levels. Also, statewide policies on language, such as the legislation which makes English the official language of the majority of states, can benefit greatly from those with knowledge of how language works and how language policies can affect people's civil rights. And you can make the case to other organizations why the knowledge and skills a linguist brings are important.

Speech language pathologist

Most of those who become speech language pathologists and work within communication sciences and disorders have some advanced training beyond a bachelor's degree. Some with degrees in linguistics who think they might want to consider becoming speech language pathologists might first become speech language pathology assistants (SLPAs). Though the requirements for SLPAs vary by state, a degree in linguistics plus some on-the-job training can sometimes suffice. The professional organization the American Speech-Language-Hearing Association (ASHA) is a good resource for more information about potential careers, internships, graduate schools, and more.

Many students combine a linguistics degree with speech language pathology training. Tracy Conner earned a BA in linguistics and then went on to get a masters degree in Speech Language Pathology. She discusses (Conner, 2016 and p.c.) how linguists are uniquely suited for SLP work, offering the following skills, abilities, and knowledge:

Linguists have extensive knowledge of linguistic systems
Linguists have reactive problem-solving skills
Linguists are good at describing/analyzing linguistic systems
Linguists can make cross-linguistic comparisons
Linguists can compare typical to disordered systems
Linguists test hypotheses
Linguists have experience of analytical reasoning
Linguists love language puzzles
Linguists enjoy interacting with people
Linguists often have experience working with consultants
Linguists have often conducted sociolinguistic interviews
Linguists have experience with other types of data elicitation

Annie, interviewed by Lauren Gawne on the *Superlinguo* blog, has a Masters of Speech Pathology; she works in schools doing assessments and therapy with primary school age kids, working with their parents, and working with teachers to make schools more inclusive for children with speech, language, and literacy needs. When Lauren asked Annie how her linguistics training helps in her job, Annie replied:

> Linguistics is a part of any speech pathology degree, but I certainly appreciated the breadth of knowledge I entered my masters with. Now, on any given day, I might be analyzing a language sample from a child, explaining linguistic concepts to teachers, or helping a group of children build their phonological awareness so they can learn to read and write.

Speech language pathology can provide direct applications of linguistics, and it's important for those involved in communication sciences and disorders to have in-depth knowledge of the study of language itself. In fact, studies suggest that children treated by speech language pathologists who have undergraduate degrees in linguistics and then pursue masters degrees in Speech Language Pathology improved faster than children treated by SLPs with only minimal linguistic preparation. (Bernhardt, 2004)

Editing and publishing, journalism

Over the last few years, there has been a lot more writing in the mainstream media about linguistics. This is likely due to there being simply more trained linguists in the world, more linguists who have realized the importance of how to communicate clearly from within the discipline to outside of it, more platforms for publication, and then more enthusiasm from traditional publishers who realize how very cool linguistics and its discoveries are! The fields of editing and publishing, as well as journalism, serve as good examples of how the broader skills of those with a linguistics background can play out in all sorts of publishing-related jobs.

Benjamin Riley, a journalist and editor, was interviewed by Lauren Gawne, of *Superlinguo*:

> There are a couple of very direct ways my linguistics degree helps in my job. A solid understanding of grammatical structures is obviously an asset in editing—it's much easier to convince an editor of something if you can back it up with jargon-y linguistic arguments. More importantly, the focus in my linguistics degree on critical analysis of all sorts of written and spoken discourse (including news media) gave me a fantastic grounding in being able to engage critically with the news I read and the news I write.

And Benjamin's summary of the broader benefits of his linguistics degree is a great example of what those who have studied linguistics say again and again:

> But really, I would say the benefits of my linguistics degree lie in its broad engagement with the humanities and social sciences. Linguistics is an incredibly diverse discipline, and studying it got me curious in so many other areas of inquiry: psychology, sociology, politics, philosophy, anthropology… the list goes on. That breadth also encourages linguistics students to think critically about what they're studying—it's hard to take so many diverse and often conflicting ways of looking at the world at face value. Curiosity and critical thinking are, I would

argue, the most important traits a journalist can possess, and studying linguistics helped me develop those in spades.

L. Phillip Lucas, an editor and copywriter, was also interviewed by Gawne, and speaks more directly to the importance of the study of language in his job as an editor:

> Any editor needs to be intimately acquainted with the nuts and bolts of language, and there's really no better way to do that than by studying linguistics… Most people see editing as a simple issue of correctness and incorrectness, but linguistics majors know better. It's actually more about making well-informed choices for appropriateness, consistency and clarity, and linguistics gives you the context to do that.

Chi Luu, Arika Okrent, John McWhorter, Ben Zimmer, Steven Pinker, and Gretchen McCulloch, among others, are linguists who write accessibly about language and linguistics for a general audience. Ben Zimmer, for example, writes language columns for *The Washington Post* and has written for other national newspapers and magazines, and is also a lexicographer (which we discuss more below).

There are even podcasts about language and linguistics, including *Lexicon Valley* and *A Way with Words*, not to mention the many linguistics blogs. Anyone can be a journalist—and some even get paid! And there are also magazines focused on language, such as the student-run *Unravel* and the LSA award-winning *Schwa Fire*.

"As an English and Linguistics major, I have found the connection between language and literature fascinating. I am planning to a pursue a career in editing and publishing, and linguistics will be central to that. I absolutely love the syntax and grammar side of linguistics; I love discovering why exactly, when I read something, a certain sentence doesn't sound right. I have also found sociolinguistics equally appealing and applicable to discussions about literature in my English courses."

Kyra is a Journalism and Linguistics major, and she when she works as an editor, she tells her writers that nearly "every rule of writing can be broken, but if you don't know the rules that you are breaking, it will show in your work." And, she adds:

> That's where a background in linguistics comes in handy. When you study the grammar of a language, you know when you can choose to omit a verb here or organize and manipulate your clauses in a certain way. I try and teach a crash-course in English grammar to familiarize writers with the rules that they already know, but don't necessarily have words for, so that they can make stylistic choices consciously. It also helps with editor-writer communication when I need to give an explanation of why something is ungrammatical.

Lexicography

Linguists can become lexicographers, those who compile and edit dictionaries. This job may conjure up images of Noah Webster or Samuel Johnson who sat alone at a desk long ago, writing *the* dictionary. But the work of dictionary making is ongoing and continuous. Language is always changing, as we know, and lexicographers must trace those changes, work to understand subtle meaning changes, and determine which words should be added to a dictionary. They conduct research across all kinds of language usage—in books, on the internet, in newspapers, everywhere there is language and text—to determine when a word is widespread and stable enough to be included in a dictionary.

And although we often say "the" dictionary, suggesting it is a kind of singular, definitive authority, there are many different dictionaries with many different goals. But the study of all aspects of linguistics is central to lexicography: phonology, morphology, syntax, and, of course, meaning.

Dictionary editors' primary job is to find and catalog the words in a language. In addition to cataloging words in well-established languages (such is the task of the *Oxford English Dictionary* or *Merriam-Webster*, for example), other lexicographers strive to catalog the words in endangered indigenous languages to help preserve those languages. Still others catalog regionalisms that might not make it into more conventional dictionaries (the *Dictionary of American Regional English*, or DARE, is a notable example).

Kori Stamper and Emily Brewster are both lexicographers at Merriam-Webster, which is known for being upfront about its descriptive attitudes towards language. They have a great collection of videos about common usage questions, which typically provide a good deal of historical explanation and linguistic analysis. Go to Merriam-Webster online and check them out!

> "If you study linguistics, you will have an awareness of language structure and use that will play out in everyday conversations and where your skills of data analysis will be useful in all sorts of ways, from figuring out where to put a comma to exploring dialectal patterns to explaining the reasons why texting will not 'ruin the language.'"

Tech industry

Like education, this field is an enormous one with so many different types of applications for those who have studied linguistics.

The most obvious ways linguists are employed within the tech industry are within Natural Language Processing and Computational Linguistics. In this subfield of linguistics, the techniques of computer science are applied to the analysis and synthesis of language; computational linguists are engaged in providing computational models of linguistic phenomena. Computational linguists develop formal models simulating aspects of human language and then develop them as computer programs. This subfield of linguistics is growing, as the applications for language and technology continue to be reimagined.

The applied work of computational linguists includes the recognition of speech by computers and smartphones and training them to get better at recognizing the unique features of their users. They also develop text-to-speech synthesizers, work on translation from one language to another by 'machines,' develop automated voice response systems and computer grammar checkers, and work to enhance web search engines, text editors, and language instruction materials.

For many jobs in computational linguistics, or natural language processing, you need to have experience in both linguistics and in programming. A few universities offer degrees in Computational Linguistics or in Natural Language Processing—and new ones are appearing—but often you need to take courses in linguistics and computer science separately. Some of the kinds of things that linguists in the NLP industry do include the following:

> Voice recognition/generation
> Information retrieval (especially search engines that do semantic searches)
> Speech synthesis
> Machine translation
> Grammar checkers
> Text classification and text clustering and other 'Big Data' applications
> Text mining—finding pieces of useful information in unstructured text
> Analyzing the language of social media

There has been work recently to develop apps for use with little-studied and endangered languages such as the 'Talking Dictionary' project of the 'Enduring Voices' project by the National Geographic or the apps and multimedia projects of the Language Conservancy.

The field of computational linguistics and natural language processing is growing like crazy, and Margaret Mitchell, a researcher at Microsoft's NLP Research Group said at a recent Linguistic Society of America meeting: "The time is right for linguists to come and start playing in NLP." And there are linguistics jobs in the software industry that do not necessarily require much programming background. On the LinguistList listserv (linguistlist.org), recent computational jobs for people with BAs in Linguistics included linguistic data manager, part of speech annotator, and speech data evaluators. Ron Kaplan, VP at Nuance Communications and Consulting Professor at Stanford, said at a Linguists in Industry panel at the LSA meeting in 2016: "From an industry point of view, this is a great time to be a linguist."

Marketing and advertising

One might not immediately put linguistics and marketing together, but it's a growing field that seems to be teeming with linguists.

An obvious niche within marketing for linguists is within branding/naming. Consider how word structure is central to creating catchy advertising terms and taglines: *drinkability* was created for Bud Light advertisements, and the blend *manscaping* became a catchword in the TV show *Queer Eye for the Straight Guy*, and popular brand names include *Swiffer* (a blend of 'sweep' and 'swift') and *Netflix* (from the clipping of 'Internet' blended with 'flicks'). *Fahrvergnugen*, from the 1990s Volkswagen advertising campaign, is a made-up compound of the German words *fahren* 'to drive,' and 'vergnugen,' which translates into something like 'enjoyment.' So *Fahrvergnugen* means 'the joy of driving a Volkswagen.' Lexicon, a company focused on product naming and branding, has been around since the early 1980s, hiring linguists whose knowledge of phonetics and phonology and of meaning—and ideally, of other languages' structures as well—is critical. Catchword is another naming/branding company that hires linguists. In these companies, marketing specialists use phonetics and sound associations to name their products. Which sounds car sounds faster—Sarrant or Tarrant? Which computer sounds more compact—Gortan or Kortan? And which product sounds more dependable—Bazia or Vazia? Researchers have found that for most English speakers (though much of the work is done cross-linguistically as well), voiceless stops (p, t, k) have a greater connotation of speed than voiced stops (b, d, g) do, fricatives (v, f, s, z) connote speed better than stops (b, p, d, t) do, voiced fricatives (v and z) connote speed better than voiceless fricative (f and s), stops (b, p, t, d) connote dependability better than fricatives (v, f, s, z), and alveolars (t, d, s, z) connote speed better than labials (p, b, f, v). A pretty cool way to apply your linguistic knowledge!

But even in marketing that is not directly concerned with phonetics, morphology, or semantics, linguists' skills are in demand. Ann Marie Olivo-Shaw, a content strategist and digital marketing professional, asks: "So why would a linguist be any good at inbound marketing? Because we know language variation." She makes the case that linguists are excellent employees to be involved in digital marketing and website design and development, as well as branding. Lisa Radding, an onomastician (someone who studies names) who is Director of Research and Product Development for a company called Ethnic Technologies, discusses (LSA, 2016) how knowledge of phonology and morphology and, of course, meaning, plays out in marketing, especially marketing to targeted groups. Their work makes use of patterns and hypothesis-testing—things that linguists are really good at. She works as a private baby name consultant too!

Anna Marie Trester of *CareerLinguist* interviews Mackenzie Warren, who works in marketing for Oxford University Press. Mackenzie writes:

> I should emphasize that it wasn't just my editorial or research experience that qualified me for this job. Proofreading skills and the ability to carry out a research initiative certainly benefit me in my work, but there is something to be said for approaching the nitty-gritty with an understanding of the larger sociocultural implications my work has. For example, a cultural studies course allowed me to delve deeply into the strategies of advertising and their effects on consumers. Several course projects on discourse analysis, intertextuality, and narrative gave me a strong understanding of online

communication and media. As important as it is to know what makes a successful marketing campaign, it is equally important to be attuned to the ways in which advertising can be problematic—e.g. issues around cultural sensitivity—and how users are expanding on and subverting the prescribed uses of media. Because I spent time studying these issues from outside the industry, I bring a perspective that isn't necessarily shared by my colleagues who come to marketing from more traditional business backgrounds.

Language documentation and revitalization

Although many newly-minted linguists like the idea of doing such important documentation and preservation work, this type of work typically grows out of community-based work conducted on a language in collaboration with speakers of the language; it is not common or practical to just 'do' language documentation work outside of academia or outside of a community's own language program.

Those interested in pursuing language documentation or revitalization are typically either members of the community whose language is endangered or those who have conducted research and worked with speakers of the language(s). A list of organizations, workshops, and community-based projects is provided on the website for this book.

As the loss of languages has become more widely acknowledged over several decades, it has grown into a social and political issue of great concern to those both within the communities whose languages are disappearing, but also to those outside of those communities. Linguists know that languages always change, and they suspect that languages have always come and gone, but the rapid rate at which languages have been decreasing over the last few hundred years, due primarily to the effects of colonization, has put an urgency behind the documentation and revitalization of many of the world's remaining languages. Some estimate that a majority of the world's languages will be gone in the next 100 years. Work on the documentation of languages with few speakers and the teaching of the languages to younger members of the community is ongoing both within those communities, as well as at academic institutions in collaborative partnerships such as the Northwest Language Institute at the University of Oregon and the American Indian Language Development Institute (AILDI) at the University of Arizona. The most effective work happens when linguists and community members work together.

Lauren Gawne of *Superlinguo* interviewed Margaret Florey, who is co-founder of the Resource Network for Linguistic Diversity and Director of a training program for documenting and revitalizing indigenous languages of Australia (DRIL). The DRIL program provides an excellent model for other revitalization and documentation programs since it "is committed to building skills in linguistics, language documentation, and language revitalisation methods so that Indigenous people can work more autonomously in their language projects." Margaret says:

> My linguistic training helps me every day! In our experience, community people value the work that linguists have done in documenting languages and preparing grammars and dictionaries. However, these materials are often impenetrable to people without linguistic training. Our training helps to make existing linguistic materials accessible, and empowers people to begin using linguistic methods themselves to document languages or to prepare resources that can be more widely used for language revitalisation activities. This work is exciting and very moving. We are privileged to be able to work every day with passionate, highly motivated, and very determined people!

Those who would like to work on the documentation and/or revitalization of endangered or little-studied languages must work within the knowledge that most languages that are endangered got that way through the ravages of colonialism. An acknowledgement of that trauma—the taking of lands, cultures, and languages—must preface any interaction with the communities affected, and coming into a community as an outsider with a savior attitude may only serve to replicate the traumas of the past.

> "I hadn't ever thought about the place of language study in relation to cultural identity, sovereignty, and civil rights; they are so completely intertwined with language. I have gained a real understanding of the links between historical events and language change, and I want others to better understand these kinds of connections."

Forensic linguistics

An emerging field at the intersection of linguistics and law is forensic linguistics. Some areas of the law that linguists typically engage with are trademark infringement, product liability, authorship of documents, and speaker identification. Forensic linguists provide expert evaluations of written items (whether on paper or onscreen) involving murders, kidnappings, fraud, and other crimes. Sometimes their expertise is so critical to a legal case that they are called upon to testify in court.

Forensic linguist Tim Grant spoke to BBC News about evidence in a case involving a terrorist suspect in the United Kingdom. He compared documents in the case to other pieces known to be written by the suspect, looking for consistent spelling and grammatical variations to see if it was likely that the suspect had written the papers. He found very close matches; that evidence contributed to the decision to charge the suspect with the crime. The suspect pleaded guilty to conspiracy to murder and was sentenced to at least 40 years in jail.

Forensic linguistics was also an essential component of the capture of the Unabomber, Theodore Kaczynski. Kaczynski's brother was the first to recognize his brother's writing style and then linguists corroborated that there were many words and phrases common in Kaczynski's known writings and the Unabomber's threat letters.

Roger Shuy is a well-known sociolinguist and forensic linguist. An example of the kind of sleuthing that he has done is his analysis of a ransom note from a kidnapping. The note featured several misspellings and the phrase "Put it in the green trash kan on the devil strip at corner 18th and Carlson." Shuy determined that the term 'devil strip' to describe the strip of grass between the sidewalk and the street was used in the area around Akron, Ohio. The police had a suspect who hailed from that geographic region who confessed to the kidnapping.

Another example comes from Claire Hardaker, a linguist at Lancaster University (United Kingdom), who was asked to help identify the masked man in a video of the murder of the U.S. journalist James Foley (who was beheaded in 2014). After analyzing the video, Hardaker suggested that the person was a native speaker of British English and likely came from the south of England, based on his vowels and the pronunciation of several words.

Not all cases are so straightforward, of course. But linguists' expertise can help police officers, attorneys, juries, and judges better understand linguistic evidence, says Lauren Johnson of *plainspokenlinguist*, "such as the likelihood that two similar trademarks will be confused by consumers or the reliability of earwitness accounts (like an eye-witness, except ear-witnesses have heard rather than seen something of possible interest)."

Polyglot jobs

Being multilingual will open up so many doors and numerous career opportunities. If you are both a polyglot and also have studied linguistics, then the world is your oyster. Career opportunities include being a translator or an interpreter, a diplomat, a humanitarian aid worker, or you can work for the CIA or the military.

Many linguistics students study other languages, develop some proficiency, and decide they'd like to work with the two (or more) languages. However, for many translation jobs—and certainly for interpreter jobs—one must have native-like fluency and reading and writing skills in the two languages. In order to be an interpreter, one must be not only completely fluent in the two languages, but also have interpretation skills, typically gained via an Interpreter Training course and test.

Knowing other languages opens up all sorts of opportunities both domestically and internationally. And if you have linguistics expertise too, that adds additional opportunities, often related to teaching, translation, software development, grammar checkers, language apps, and so on. In fact, almost all of the career opportunities discussed in this chapter are enhanced if you are bilingual or multilingual.

Monika received BAs in both Linguistics and Political Science. Her expertise and work on Latvian led to her job doing interpreting work for the U.S. military. Lauren Gawne of *Superlinguo* interviewed Monika about her work as an applied linguist deployed to Latvia with the U.S. Army for Operation Atlantic Resolve.

> Because of the diverse nature of the job, doing anything from translating ancient naughty poems to working with interrogators, different subfields of linguistics come into play. Quickly analyzing the semantics and meaning behind a comment is necessary for the collection of information, as opposed to a word-for-word translation. Studying semiotics also helps greatly, as symbols, signs, and gestures can be interpreted differently in other cultures and languages. Having this information allows for avoiding uncomfortable situations or having conversations halted due to a misinterpretation of signs. Syntax training and, I hate to say it, drawing syntax trees, prepared me to be able to instantly translate from SVO languages (English) to a language with relatively free word order (Latvian), to be able to mentally break apart a phrase, switch it around, and have a coherent translated phrase come out.

"Language is such an integral component of how humans interact and engage with the world around us, and what better way to appreciate the people around us than by engaging in learning other languages and in truy understanding how they work?"

Monika also adds these important words:

> I wish that it had been emphasized just how versatile and broadly applicable a degree in Linguistics can be, and not just as a stepping stone for academia or an MA program. Being able to work as a journalist, teacher, translator/interpreter, editor, writer, or even in public relations or the field of intelligence, is something I don't think ever gets discussed in the classroom in terms of linguistic jobs in the 'real world'.

Lauren Gawne also interviewed Nicole Rodgrigues, "a Brazilian translator who specializes in translating, localizing and transcreating web and mobile content from English to Brazilian Portuguese. She is also a content curator and the official translator for Tumblr in Brazil." This is another great example of the intersection of linguistics with translation and the tech industry.

Nicole writes:

> My job is to understand what exactly that ad creator wanted the audience to feel and to adapt it, or even rewrite it, so that it will look like it was written in Brazil and for Brazil. And, often, this process will not only involve the adaptation of the text, but of the images, graphics, and colors used in the ad as well. I am not responsible for recreating the other elements of the ad, apart from the text, but it is my job to point out that a certain color, image or symbol can be considered offensive, vulgar, or dubious in our culture, so that the advertising agency has the chance to change it to something that will suit the target market best.

The CIA and the FBI recruit linguists and polyglots. And a background in linguistics can lead to international work in various capacities. For example, *Superlinguo*'s Lauren Gawne, interviewed Hugh, a humanitarian aid worker, who travels to countries after a disaster to help set up humanitarian assistance programs.

> My education in general, but specifically linguistics, taught me how to think critically… I am able to reflect back on what I am

doing and consider if it is the approach to doing something, if a project is having some other unintended consequence, might there be a better way to achieve the same result. More concretely, linguistics… gave me an introduction to social sciences, which is the foundation of the data gathering and analysis work I do. Coming at this strictly from a stats background would have been a challenge, because none of the data quite fit the idealised mathematical world I was initially trained in. It's also helped with learning bits of new languages, and with working in a highly multicultural environments, for I'm able to understand why people don't understand each other.

> "Studying linguistics has helped me to (1) analyze languages without prior knowledge of those languages, (2) analyze a language without having to learn it, (3) find patterns and structure within something unfamiliar, and (4) learn another language far easier."

Lots of other things!

And the list of the kinds of jobs that linguists have could go on and on, from the dialect coaches who work with actors on accents to cross-cultural and cross-linguistic consultants, to jobs not yet imagined. But linguists are also lawyers, doctors, librarians, bankers, bakers, and candlestick makers. And the study of linguistics doesn't necessarily have to play out in what you do for a job in a direct way, but rather it can and will shape who you are and how you interact with the world.

Linguistics is the scientific study of language, but the effects of the research are applied in a variety of ways, many of which we have seen in the previous section with the numerous examples of people with some training in linguistics engaged in diverse jobs and careers around the world. Some of these are the more obvious traditional 'language-related' careers, which include many of the jobs we discussed above, but now that we have been doing more follow-up with linguistics graduates and now that there are just more different kinds of jobs out there, it's exciting to see the many and diverse ways in which those who have studied linguistics can apply their knowledge and skills.

Students who study linguistics acquire valuable intellectual skills, such as analytical reasoning, critical thinking, argumentation, and clarity of expression. They can make insightful observations, formulate clear and testable hypotheses, generate predictions, make arguments and draw conclusions, and communicate findings to a wider community. Linguistics students are therefore well equipped for a variety of graduate-level and professional programs and careers.

Studying linguistics will have applications beyond just jobs, though; it will have applications to nearly everything you do.

- You will truly understand and appreciate the liberal arts, and the connections between humanities and social sciences.
- You will be a master of critical thinking and analysis.
- You will truly understand scientific inquiry and what it means to 'do science.'
- You will be a better scholar of human behavior.
- You will appreciate and celebrate diversity of languages, peoples, and cultures.

A survey conducted by the Association of American Colleges and Universities in 2013 found that:

- More than nine in ten of those surveyed say it is important that those they hire demonstrate ethical judgment and integrity; intercultural skills; and the capacity for continued new learning.
- More than three in four employers say they want colleges to place more emphasis on helping students develop five key learning outcomes, including: critical thinking, complex problem-solving, written and oral communication, and applied knowledge in real-world settings.

- Employers endorse several educational practices as potentially helpful in preparing college students for workplace success. These include practices that require students to:
  a) conduct research and use evidence-based analysis;
  b) gain in-depth knowledge in the major and analytic, problem-solving, and communication skills; and
  c) apply their learning in real-world settings.

Studying linguistics is the perfect way to develop these practices, skills, and expertise! And we firmly believe that learning about language as linguists do is so very important—the study of language is quite simply something that everyone should know about. Language is what makes us human, and it's immensely interesting and important. Have fun!

References

Adger, C., Snow, C., & Christian, D. (2002/2018). *What teachers need to know about language.* Washington, DC: Delta Systems.

Bernardt, B. (2004). Editorial: Maximizing success in phonological intervention. *Child Language Teaching and Therapy, 20*(3), 195–198.

Charity Hudley, A.H., & Mallinson, C. (2014). *We do language: English language variation in the secondary English classroom.* New York, NY: Teachers College Press.

Conner, T. (2016). Speech pathology. Presentation at the American Dialect Society annual meeting, Washington, DC.

Denham, K., & Lobeck, A. (Eds.) (2005). *Language in the schools: Integrating linguistic knowledge into K-12 education.* Mahwah, NJ: Lawrence Erlbaum Associates.

Denham, K., & Lobeck, A. (Eds.) (2010). *Linguistics at school: Language awareness in primary and secondary education.* New York, NY: Cambridge University Press.

Denham, K., & Pippin, D. (2018). *Voices of the Pacific Northwest: Language and life along the Columbia and throughout Cascadia from the 18th century to the present, a curriculum of historical and linguistic inquiry.* Retrieved June 17, 2018 from www.voicesofthepnw.net.

Higgins, C. (n.d.). *Talking story about Pidgin: Exploring the creole language of Hawai'i.* Retrieved June 6, 2018 from www.sls.hawaii.edu/pidgin/

Honda, M. (1994). Linguistic inquiry in the science classroom: "It is science, but it's not like a science problem in a book." *MIT Occasional Papers in Linguistics 6*. Cambridge, MA: MITWPL.

LSA (2017). *The state of linguistics in higher education: Annual report 2017. Fifth edition, Issued February 2018*. Retrieved June 17, 2018 from www.linguisticsociety.org/sites/default/files/Annual_Report_2017_Final_2.pdf

Radding, L. (2016). Linguists in industry. Presentation at the Linguistic Society of America annual meeting, Washington, DC.

Reaser, J., Adger, C.T., Wolfram, W., & Christian, D. (2017). *Dialects at school: Educating linguistically diverse students*. New York, NY: Routledge.

Rickford, J. (1999). *African American Vernacular English: Features and use, evolution, and educational implications.* Oxford, UK: Blackwell.

Roh, A. (2010). And you can all say haboo: Enriching the standard language arts curriculum with linguistic analysis. In Denham, C. & Lobeck, A. (Eds.), *Linguistics at school: Language awareness in primary and secondary education* (pp. 234–239). New York, NY: Cambridge University Press.

Wheeler, R., & Swords, R. (2004). Codeswitching: Tools of language and culture transform the dialectally diverse classroom. *Language Arts*, *81*(6), 1–11.

Index

Note: Page numbers in *italics* refer to figures. Page numbers in **bold** refer to tables.

absolutive case 71
accents 26, 48, 60–61, 139, 142–145, 150
accusative case 70–71, 129
acoustic phonetics 54
acrolect (higher prestige) 140
adjective phrases (AP) *88*
adjectives *73–75*, 76–77, 109
adverbs 76–**77**
advertising, careers in 198–200
affixes: definition of 22, 64; derivational 66, 67, *73*, *74*, 85, 86; inflectional 66–72, *74–75*, 79–80, 86, 129–130, 132; in word trees (Aff) *72–75*
African American English (AAE) 11–12, 48, 79–80, 135, 142, 147
Aleut (language) 44–45
allophones 56
allthingslinguistic (blog) 187
alphabets 10, 57
alveolars 49, *50*, 52–53, 123, 169, 199
ambiguity 21, 75, *91–92*, 105, 107–108, 171–*173*
amelioration in word meaning 131

American Dialect Society Word of the Year candidates (2017) 76–77
American English *see* English
American Sign Language (ASL) 66, 72, 163
American Speech-Language-Hearing Association (ASHA) 191
analytic languages 79–80, 81, 86, 100, 130
animacy 69–70, 79
animal communication 6–9
anomalous sentences 20, 109–111, 172–174, *174*, *173*
antonyms 104–105, 118
aphasia 166–169, *167*, 169–170
Appalachian dialects 11, 146–147
a-prefix 146–147
arbitrariness (design feature) 8
articulation, places and manner of 23, *24*, 49–52, *50*, *51*, *143*
articulatory phonetics 48–52, *50*, *51*, 62
aspiration (puff of air) 55–56
assertions 117–118
assimilation of sounds 25, 52–53

Association of American Colleges and Universities survey 207–208
"association time" 170–171
auditory cortex (brain) 164–165
auditory phonetics 54
auxiliary verbs 42, **78**, 80, 96–97, 133

/b/ 49–51, *50*, 53
backformation 23, 64, 76, 134
basilect (less prestige) 140
Baudelaire, Charles 106–107
Baugh, John 150
Bengali (language) 72
Beowulf 13–14
Berber (language) 32–33
Berko Gleason, Jean 53
be verb in AAE 11, 79–80
biases about language 135, 147–151, 174–175
bilabials 49–51, *50*, 52–53, 199
bilingualism 151, 153, 169–70, 176, 186–188, 203–206
blends 22, 64, 76, 77, 198
blogs 187, 192, 194
borrowing for new words 34–35, 59–60, 130
bound morphemes 65, 72
brain: impaired language in 166–169, *167*, 169–170; language localization in *167*; left and right hemispheres of 164–166, *166*, 166–167, *167*, 169; research tools and methods 164, 170–171, 173–175, *174*; sounds, processing by 54, 164–165
branding/naming 198
Brewster, Emily 196
British English 139, 144, 203
broadening of meaning 131
Broca, Paul 164
Broca's aphasia 166–169, *167*
Brown, Roger 158

California Vowel Shift 144
Canadian Vowel Shift 144
Canterbury Tales, The (Chaucer) 14
CareerLinguist 199
career options: with editing 193–195; with endangered languages 200–202; in forensics 202–203; as lexicographer 195–196; in marketing 198–200; mentions of 63, 83, 103, 119, 153, 175–176, 179, 206; for multilingual people 203–206; with non-profits 190–191; as speech language pathologist 176, 191–192; with teaching 181–188; in tech industry 196–98; with TESOL 186–188; with testing agencies 188–190
cases for nouns 70–71
Center for Applied Linguistics (CAL) 190
changes in language *see* historical linguistics, topics in
Chaucer, Geoffrey 14, 131
child language acquisition *see* first language acquisition
Chinese 10, 45, 61, 79, 152
Chomsky, Noam 2, 5, 20, 155
Christopher (linguistic savant) 32–33
circumfixes 67, 68
classifiers for nouns 72, 78
clauses 87–88, 93–94, 131–132, 162, 172–173
clipping 22, 64, 76, 198
clitics 82
closed class words 77
coda in syllables 57–*59*
cognates 123
colonialism 11, 33, 200, 201–202
communities of practice 11–12
community colleges 182–183
comparative method of language change 122–128, 135

compounding 23, 34, 64, 130
Computational Linguistics 196–198
conjunctions 39–42, *42*, **78**
Conner, Tracy 191–192
connotations of words 105
consonants: clusters of 25, 58–*59*; of English 49, *50*; in IPA *24*, 49; stops 49–51, *50*, 55–56, 123, 169, 199; in syllables *57–59*; voicing in 49–51, *50*, 52, 53, 55–56, 199; *see also specific consonants*
contact languages 33–36
content words 76–**77**, 168
context, for meaning *see* pragmatics, topics in
context effect 171
conversation, maxims of 112–114, 119
conversational implicature 112, 119
cooperative principle (for conversations) 114, 119
corpus callosum 165
Correspondences (Baudelaire) 106–107
creaky voice 145, 150
creole languages 33–36, **36**, 79, 134, 140, 153, 164, 184, 185

data, in scientific method 28, 37–43, 43–46
Deaf community and signing 5, 66, 72, **127**, 157, 161–164, 165
definiteness 68, 71, 77
deletion (syntax) 18, 98–99, 102
deletion of sound 25, 54
Denham, Kristin 185
denotations of words 105
derivational affixes 66, 67, 73, *74*, 85, 86
descriptive grammar 27–30
design features of language 7–9

determiners 77, **78**, *88–93*
diachronic linguistics 15, 16, 121, 138; *see also* historical linguistics, topics in
dialects: accents in 26, 48, 60–61, 139, 142–145, 150; vs. languages 10; in literature 183–184; official policies toward 151–152; regional factors in 10–11, 26, 139–143, *141*, *143*; social factors in 10–12, 29–30, 135, 143–145, 146–151; word differences in 140
dictionaries 15, 76, 77, 83, 195–196, 197
discreteness (design feature) 8
discrimination in language use 136, 147–151, 153, 190
displacement (design feature) 8–9
dissimilation in sounds 53
distinctive sound variations 55
documentation of languages 200–202
Documenting and Revitalizing Indigenous Languages of Australia (DRIL) 201
duration of sound 54–55, 60
Dutch 10, 122–124, *124*, *126*
Dyirbal (Australia) 71, 79

Early Modern English **13**, 133, 139
Eckert, Penelope 144–145
-ed suffix 35, 86, 145, 159
editing, careers in 193–195
education *see* teaching
Educational Linguistics 186
Educational Testing Service (ETS) 188–190
eggcorn mispronunciations 23
ellipsis (deletion) 18, 98–99, 102
employers, survey of 207–208
endangered languages 197, 200–202
England 14, 27, 136, 139, 142, 203

English: articulation of sounds of
48–52, *50*, *51*, 53, 55–56, *143*;
attitudes about usage of 15,
27–28, 29–30, 136, 147–151,
152; British 139, 142, 144, 203;
dialects *see* dialects; inflectional
affixes in 66–67, **67**, 68, 70, 86;
intonation in 61–62; language
changes in 12–15, **13**, **67**,
102–103, *126*, 129–134, 146;
language family of 122–124,
124, *126*; "official" 152, 153,
191; syllables in 57–61, *59*;
wh-question formation in 38–43,
41, *42*, 62, 95, 96, 132–133,
160–162
English Language
Amendment 152
English Language Learners (ELL)
186–188
English teaching 153, 183–188
entailment 21, 108, 112,
115–116, 118
epilepsy 165, 169
ergative case 71
*Ethnologue: Languages of the
World* (Gordon) 122, **127**
Event-Related (Brain) Potentials
(ERPs) 173–174, *174*
experimental techniques 171
external language change 128
eye-tracking 170

/f/ 49, *50*
Fahrvergnugen 198
felicity conditions (of speech acts)
117–118, 119
figurative language 105–107
Finnish 55, 60, 71
first language acquisition: of any
language 160–161, 163–164;
of challenging sounds 48, 52;
critical period for 156–157, 163,
169; effect on brain hemispheres
165, 169; of grammatical
rules 158–161; of indigenous
languages 128; with innate
knowledge 32, 53, 155–156, 158,
163; and language change 134;
stages of 31, 158–159; as testing
ground for theories 134, 160–162,
164; with words 60, 83
Florey, Margaret 201
fluent aphasia 168
Foley, James 203
forensic linguistics 202–203
Frameworks Institute 190–191
free morphemes 65
French: comparisons to other
languages 25, 43–44, 69, 96–97,
107, 124, *126*; influence on
other languages 14, 33, 35, 130;
protection of 15; varieties of
10, 149
fricatives 49, *50*, 54,
123, 199
function words 77–78, **78**, 168

Gallaudet University 163
Gawne, Lauren 192, 193, 194, 201,
204, 205
gender, grammatical 68–69, 71,
129, 183
gender bias 145, 150, 174–175
generation, language 161–164
generative linguistics 5
genitive case 129
German 51, 52, 68, 69, 71, 92–93,
107, 122–124, *124*, *126*, 161
Germanic languages 121, 122–124,
124, 125–126, *126*
Gordon, Raymond G. 122, **127**
Gothic *124*, **125**
grammar: definition of 5,
20–26, 27, 46; descriptive and
prescriptive 27–30; linguistic vs.
"school" 20, 26, 27–30, 85–87;
and mental grammar 30, 99,
102; and Universal Grammar
(UG) 30–36

grammatical information in words 66–72, 77, 79–80, 100, 129–130, 132
Grant, Tim 202
GRE (Graduate Record Exam) 189
Great Vowel Shift 131
Greek 32, 121, **125**, *126*
Grice, Paul 113–114

Haitian Creole 35–36, **36**
Hardaker, Claire 203
Hawaii 152, 153
Hawaiian Creole English (Pidgin) 35–36, **36**, 153, 185
Hayakawa, S.I. 152
head (of phrase) 87, 89
hierarchical structures *74, 89–90, 101*
Higgins, Christina 185
historical linguistics, topics in: attitudes toward change 15, 136; benefits of study of 135–136; comparative method 122–128, 135; early developments 121–122; English language changes 12–15, **13, 67**, 102–103, *126*, 129–134, 146; language families 122–128, *126*, **127**, 127–128; overview of 15; reasons for language change 133–135; types of language change 128–133, 135
Hixkaryana *93–94*
Hmong 119, **127**
Hockett, Charles 7
Hoffman, Mika 189
homophones 105, 143, 168
Honda, Maya 185–186
humanitarian aid, career in 205–206
hypothesis in scientific method 37–38, 40–43, 44–45

identity through language 10, 135, 147
Idioma de Señas de Nicaragua (ISN) 162–164
idioms 107
imperatives (commands) 117
indigenous language families (American) 127–128
Indo-European languages 78, 122, **125**, 125–127, *126*
infixes 67–68
inflectional affixes 66–72, **67**, 68, *74–75*, 79–80, 86, 129–130, 132
-*ing* rule with *a*-prefix 146–147
inquiry, scientific 5, 28, 36–43, 43–46, 160–162, 170–175, 184, 185–186
insertion of sound 25, 54
intensity of sound 54, 60
interdental fricatives *50*, 54, 123, 199
internal language change 128–129
International Phonetic Alphabet (IPA) 23, *24*, 34–35, 49–52, *50*, *51*, 56
interpreting, careers in 203–205
interrogatives 39–45, 95, 117
intonation 61–62, 109
Inuktitut (language) 67–68
ISN (Idioma de Señas de Nicaragua) 162–164
Italian 15, 100, 124, *136*

Japanese 52, *59*–60, 69, 92–93, 100, 119, 165
Jeantel, Rachel 150–151
Johnson, Lauren 203
Johnson, Samuel 15
Jones, William 121–122
journalism, careers in 193–195

K12 teaching 153, 183–187
Kaczynski, Theodore 202

Kaplan, Ron 198
Kegl, Judy 163
Keyser, Beth 184
Korean 52, 56, 69, 78, 100, 119, 123

labiodental fricatives 49, *50*, 54, 199
Labov, William 143–144
language: acquisition of *see* first language acquisition; vs. animal communication 6–9; and brain *see* psycholinguistics, topics in; change in *see* historical linguistics, topics in; control of 15, 27–28, 29–30, 136, 151–152; definitions 6, 15–16; human capacity for 30–36, 155, 161, 163; identity through 10, 135, 147; intuitive, unconscious knowledge about 16–19, 20, 155, 170; planning and policies for 151–152, 191; rules of *see* grammar; variation in 3–4, 9–12; *see also* sociolinguistics, topics in
language arts teaching 153, 183–186
Language Instinct, The (Pinker) 136
languages: comparisons between 43–45, 78–79, 96, 102, 106, 122–128, 135; differences with sounds 25, 51, 52, 55–56, 61, 165; endangered 197, 200–202; families of 122–128, *126*, **127**, 127–128; influence between 134–135; number of 122, **127**, 127–128; types, by word order 92–95, *93*, *94*; types, by word structure 3, 79–81, 83, 100
laryngealization 145, 150
Latin 60, 121, 124–125, **125**, *126*

Latvian 204
left hemisphere language dominance 164–166, *166*, 166–167, *167*, 169
Lenneberg, Eric 155–156
lexical ambiguity 21, 75, 91, 105, 171–172
lexical categories 76–77, **77**, 167–168
lexical decision task 170–171
lexicography 83, 195–196
lexicon (mental) 66, 74, 83, 155, 170
linguistic competence and performance 19, 20
linguistic profiling 150–151
linguistics: benefits of studying 192, 193, 205, 206, 207–208; book overview 1–4; degrees in 179, *180–182*, *181*, 184–185, 186, 197; and other disciplines 155, 178, 193, 197; overview of 5–6, 46, 206–207; and scientific inquiry 5, 28, 36–43, 43–46, 160–162, 170–175, 184, 185–186; *see also* career options
LinguistList listserv 198
literature, study of 183–184, 194
Logical Structure of Linguistic Theory, The (Chomsky) 5
low back merger (vowels) 142–143, *143*
Lucas, L. Phillip 194
Lushootseed (language) 64, 79

/m/ 49, *50*, 51, 52
McCulloch, Gretchen 187
MacDonald, Jennifer 187–188
magazines, on linguistics 194
Mandarin 10, 61, 78, 92, 152
marketing, careers in 198–200
Martin, Trayvon 150–151
maxims of conversation 112–114
Mead, Margaret 34

meaning, study of *see* pragmatics, topics in; semantics, topics in
mental grammar 30, 99, 102
Merriam-Webster Dictionary 76, 77, 196
metaphors 105–106
metathesis (switching) 25, 53, 134
metonymy 106
Middle English **13**, 13–15, 103, 121, *126*, 130, 131, 133
Mitchell, Margaret 197
Mohawk 78–79, 101
monolinguals 170
monomorphemic words 65–66
morphemes 22, 64, 65–66, 72, 82, 125
morphology, topics in: benefits of study of 82–83; categories of words, syntactic 39, 76–79, **77**, **78**, 83, 85–87, 89, 102, 147; change in language 83, 129–130; definition 3, 22, 64–65, 82; derivational affixes 66, 67, 73, *74*, 85, 86; inflectional affixes 66–72, *74–75*, 79–80, 86, 129–130, 132; language typologies 3, 79–81, 83, 100; morphemes 22, 64, 65–66, 72, 82, 125; new word formation 22–23, 34, 64, 66, 76–79, 83, 130, 134, 198; syntax, overlap with 70, 76–79, 83, 85, 99–102; unconscious knowledge of rules 22–23, 65, *74*, 81; variations in language 83, 145–146; word boundaries 60, 64–65, 81–82; word trees *72–75*
morphosyntax 76, 85, 99–102
movement rules (word order) 18, 39, 95–98, *98*, 102
mutual intelligibility 10

/ŋ/ 49, *50*
N400 effect 173–174

naming/branding 198
narrowing of meaning 131
National Fair Housing Alliance (NFHA) 150
"national" language 151–152
natural language changes 133–134
Natural Language Processing (NLP) 196, 197
Navajo 61, 69–70, 79
negation 27, 29–30, 77, 115–116, 132–133
negative face and politeness 116
New York City department stores 143–144
Nicaraguan Sign Language 162–164
nominative case 70–71, 129
non-fluent aphasia 168
non-profit organizations 190–191
non-rhotic dialects 142
Norman French 14, 130
North American Computational Linguistics Olympiad (NACLO) 186
Northern California Vowel Shift 144
Northern Cities Vowel Shift 144–145
noun phrases in structure trees (NP) 40–*42*, *88–94*, *98*, *101*, *173*
nouns: grammatical markers for 70–72, 129; in Old English 129; syntax category of 61, 76–77, **77**, 78–79, 85–86; in word trees (N) *72–74*
nucleus in syllables *57*, *59*, 62
null subject languages 32–33, 100

objects *see* word order of language typologies
Official English laws 152, 153, 191
Old English **13**, 13–14, 53, **67**, 102, *126*, 129–132, 134, 146
Olivo-Shaw, Ann Marie 199
O'Neil, Wayne 185–186

onset in syllables 57–59
open class words 76–77, 167
OVS languages 92, *93–94*

/p/ 49, *50*, 55–56
P600 effect 173–174, *174*
paraphrases 108
parts of speech 39–42, *42*, 61, 76, 85, 146, 183, 198
passive voice 95–96, 168
past tense 34–35, 42, 66–68, 77, 79–80, 86, 145–146, 159
pejoration in word meaning 131
personification 107
PhD programs 181–182, *182*, 186
phonemes *50*, 56, 168–169
phonetics and phonology, topics in: associations with sounds 171, 198–199; benefits of study of 62–63; definitions of 3, 20, 23; inventory of possible sounds 23–25, *24*; with IPA transcription 23, *24*, 34–35, 49–52, *50*, *51*, 63; language change 62, 123–125, **125**, 130–131; meaningful distinctions of sounds 54–56, 61–62; perception of sounds 54; production of sounds 48–52, *50*, *51*, 62; rules for pronunciation 52–54, 63; stress patterns 25–26, 55–56, 58, 60–61, 62, 63, 81; syllable structures 56–60; with tone and intonation 25, 61–62, 109, 130, 155; unconscious knowledge of rules 23, 25–26, 53, 56, 57, 58, 59, 63; use of // and [] 23, 56
phrase structure in syntax *41–42*, 87–94, *94*, *98*, *101*
pidgin languages 33–36, **36**, 79, 134, 153, 184, 185
PIE (Proto-Indo-European) 122, **125**, 125–127, *126*
Pinker, Steven 136, 163

Pippin, David 185–186
pitch of sound 54, 60, 61–62, 165
plainspokenlinguist blog 203
planning and policies for language 151–152, 191
plurals 25, 53, 67, *74*, 129, 159
podcasts, on linguistics 194
poetry, syllable-based 57
politeness 116–117, 119
polyglots, careers for 203–206
polymorphemic words 65
polysemy 105, 118
polysynthetic languages 80–81, 85, 100–101
Portuguese 25, 33, 107, 124, *126*, 205
positive face and politeness 116
post-vocalic [r] 142, 143–144
pragmatics, topics in: benefits of study of 119; definition 3, 104, 112; politeness 116–117; presuppositions 115–16; rules for conversation 112–114; speech acts 112, 117–118, 119; *see also* semantics, topics in
prairie dogs 7–9
predicates *88*, 109; *see also* verb phrases (VP)
predictions, in scientific method 37–38, 40–43, 45
prefixes 22, 64, 65–66, 67, 68, *73–74*, 146–147
prepositional phrases (PP) 40–41, *41*, *88–92*, 110
prepositions 35, 39–41, *41*, **78**
prescriptive grammar 27–30, 136
Present Day English (PDE) 12–15, **67**, 129–133
preservation of languages 200–202
prestige in language use 136, 140, 143–144, 190
presuppositions 115–116
"priming" of words 170–171
productivity (design feature) 8

pronunciation *see* phonetics and phonology, topics in
Proto-Indo-European (PIE) 122, **125**, 125–127, *126*
psycholinguistics, topics in: benefits of study of 175–176; brain impairment and language research 166–169, *167*, 169–170; brain responses to anomalous sentences 172–174, *174*, *173*; brain's left and right hemispheres 164–166, *166*, 166–167, *167*, 169–170; definition 4, 155, 175; generation of ISN 162–164; methodologies for 170–172; processing of sounds 54, 164–165; *see also* first language acquisition

quantifier scope 22
question formation 38–45, *41*, *42*, 61–62, 95–97, 132–133, 160–162

/ɹ/ ("r" in English): articulation of *50*–51, 131; in child language acquisition 48; and /l/ 52; post-vocalic 26, 142, 143–144
Radding, Lisa 199
Reaser, Jeffrey 185
reconstructed language 125, 127
recursion *89–90*, 102
reduplication 34, 64
regional variations 10–11, 26, 139–143, *141*, *143*
relative clauses 172–*173*
rental properties, discrimination with 150
repetition effect 171
research career opportunities *181*, 181–182, 190, 195–196, 199–200, 202–203
research tools and methods, brain 164, 170–171, 173–175, *174*
revitalization of languages 200–202

Right Ear Advantage 165–166, *166*
Riley, Benjamin 193–194
rime in syllables 57–59, *59*
Rodrigues, Nicole 205
Roh, Angela 183–184
Romance languages 80, 82, 121, 125
root morphemes 65, 72, 82, 125
Royal Asiatic Society 121

/s/ 25, 49, *50*, 53, 54, 159
Sanskrit 69, 121, **125**, *126*
schools, K12 153, 183–187
scientific method 5, 28, 36–43, 43–46, 161–162, 170–175, 184, 185–186
second language learning 157–158
selectional restrictions 109
semanticity (design feature) 7
semantics, topics in: ambiguity 21, 75, 91, 105, 171–172; benefits of study of 118–119; brain research with 171–172, 173–*174*; definition 3, 20, 104, 112, 118; figurative language 105–107, 118; language change 14–15, 131; sentence meanings 107–111, 118; sound and meaning 55, 61–62, 109, 150; syntax, overlap with 20, 109–111, 118, 172–174, *173*, *174*; unconscious knowledge of rules 20–22; *see also* pragmatics, topics in
semiotics 204
sentence structure: intonation and 62; in phrase structure trees (S) *41*–*42*, *87*–*94*, *98*, *101*, 172–173, *173*; *see also* syntax, topics in
sentence types and speech acts 117–118
Shuy, Roger 203
sign languages 5, 66, 72, **127**, 157, 162–164, 165
slips of the tongue 19, 171

Index 219

Smith, Neil 32
social studies teaching 185
sociolinguistics, topics in:
 benefits of study of 138–139,
 153, 199–200; definition 12,
 138–139; discrimination in
 language use 136, 147–151, 153,
 190; grammatical variations
 145–147; policy and planning,
 language 151–152, 191; regional
 variations 10–11, 26, 139–143,
 141, 143; sound variations
 (accents) 26, 48, 60–61, 139,
 142–145; stigma in language
 choices 11–12, 29–30, 135,
 143–145, 147–151; syntactic
 variations 103, 146–147
sounds of language *see* phonetics
 and phonology, topics in
Southern dialects 142, 143,
 147
SOV languages 45, 92–*94*,
 131–132
Spanish 32, 51, 52, 80, 82, 124,
 126, 149
speech acts 112, 117–118, 119
speech errors 19, 171
speech language pathologists
 (SLPAs) 176, 191–192
split-brain patients 165
Sranan (creole language) **36**
Stamper, Kori 196
stigma in language use 11–12,
 29–30, 135, 143–145, 147–151
stops (consonants) 49–51, *50*,
 55–56, 123, 169, 199
stress, patterns of 25–26, 55–56,
 58, 60–61, 62, 63, 81
subjects of sentence 32–33, 70–71,
 88, 92–96, 109–111; *see also* word
 order of language typologies
subject-verb agreement
 99–100
substrate and superstrate
 languages (pidgins) 33–35

suffixes 22, 60, 64, 65–66, 67,
 111, 129
Superlinguo (blog) 192, 193, 201,
 204, 205
survey of employers 207–208
SVO languages 34–35, 43–45, 86,
 92–94, *94*, 95–98, *98*, 131–132
Swahili 60, 80, 100, 123
Swedish 10, 69, 122–124, *124, 126*
syllable structures 56–60
synchronic study of language
 15, 138
synesthesia 106–107
synonyms 104–5, 108, 118, 130
syntactic categories of words 39,
 76–79, **77, 78**, 83, 85–87, 89,
 102, 147
syntax, topics in: ambiguity 21,
 91–92, 107–108, 172–173, *173*;
 benefits of study of 102–103;
 brain research with 173–
 174, *174*; change in language
 102–103, 131–133; definition 3,
 16, 85, 87, 102; hierarchies and
 recursion *89–90*, 102; inquiry
 on question formation
 38–45, *41, 42*, 61–62,
 160–162; language typologies
 by word order 92–95, *93, 94*;
 morphology, overlap with 70,
 76, 85, 99–102; movement
 rules for word order 18, 39,
 95–98, *98*, 102; notation
 conventions 87–88; phrase
 structure rules *41–42*, 87–
 94, *94, 98, 101*, 172–173, *173*;
 semantics, overlap with 20, 109–
 11, 172–174, *174, 173*; syntactic
 categories of words 39, 76–79,
 77, 78, 83, 85–87, 89, 102, 147;
 unconscious knowledge of
 rules 16–19, 87, 91, 99, 102;
 "understood elements" rule 17,
 18, 98–99, 102; variations in
 language 146–147

synthetic languages 79–80, 100, 129, 131–132

Tagalog (language) 8, 68
teaching: about linguistics 181–186; vs. acquisition of first language 158–160; in K12 schools 153, 183–187; sign language 163; TESOL 186–188; at universities 181–182, *182*, 187
Teaching English to Speakers of Other Languages (TESOL) 186–188
tech industry, careers in 196–198
tenses, verb 34–35, 42, 66–68, 77, 79–80, 145, 159
testing agencies 188–190
Thai 61, 165
/θ/ 48, *50*, 52, 123
/ð/ 48, *50*, 52
thematic roles (semantic) 110–111
theoretical or formal linguistics 36–37
theories, construction of 5, 28, 36–43, 43–46, 160–162, 170–175, 184, 185–186
Tok Pisin (creole language) 34–35
tones 25, 61–62, 130, 165
tongue as articulator 48, 49, *50*, 51
translation, careers in 203, 205
Trester, Anna Marie 199
Tsimpli, Ianthi-Maria 32

Unabomber letters 202
United Kingdom 202, 203
United States: dialect regions in 11, 26, 139–143, *141*; official language in 152–153
Universal Grammar (UG) 31–36
universities: degree programs at 179, *180–182*, *181*, 184–185, 186; teaching and research at 181–182, *182*, 184, 185–186

U.S. Army, work for 204–205
U.S. Court Interpreters Act of 1978 151
U.S. Voting Rights Act of 1975 151

"Valley Girl" speech 144–145
variation in language 3–4, 9–12; *see also* sociolinguistics, topics in
verb phrases (VP) *41–42*, *88–94*, *98*, *101*, *173*
verbs: auxiliary 42, **78**, 80, 96–97, 133; *be* in AAE 11, 79–80; as complete sentences 100–101; -*ing* forms with *a*-prefix 146–147; movement rule with 95–97; in Old English 129–130; semantic criteria for 109–110; strong and weak 129–130; syntax category of 61, 76–77, **77**, 78, 85–86; tenses of 34–35, 42, 66–68, 77, 79–80, 86, 145–146, 159; transitive and intransitive 70–71; in word trees (V) *72*, *74–75*; *see also* word order of language typologies
vervet monkeys 7–9
vocal cords 49, 53
vocal fry 145, 150
voicing in consonants 49–51, *50*, 52, 53, 55–56, 199
vowels: chart of English *51*, *143*; dialectal mergers of 142–143, *143*; distinctive variations of 55, 143; in IPA *24*; past tense forms with 145; shifts of 131, 144–145; in syllables *57–59*
VSO languages 92, *94*, 95–98, *98*

Warlpiri 111
Warren, Mackenzie 199–200
Washington State University 185
Welsh 94, 97–98, *126*
Wernicke, Karl 166–167

Wernicke's aphasia *167*, 167–169
Western Washington University 184–185
wh-question formation 38–45, *41*, *42*, 62, 95, 96, 132–133, 160–162
Wolfram, Walt 185
word boundaries and recognition 60, 64–65, 81–82, 170–171
word differences, dialectal 140
word formation (new) 22–23, 34, 64, 66, 76–79, 83, 130, 134, 198
word meanings *see* semantics, topics in
word order of language typologies: in language change 131–132; movement rules for 18, 39, 95–98, *98*, 102; overview of 92–95, *93*, *94*; with OVS 92, *93–94*; with SOV 45, 92–94, *94*, 131–132; with SVO 34–35, 43–45, 86, 92–94, *94*, 95–98, *98*, 131–132; with VSO 92, *94*, 95–98, *98*
word structure *see* morphology, topics in
writing, careers in 193–195
writing systems 10, 57

Yup'ik 80–81, 82, 100

/z/ 25, *50*, 53
Zimmer, Ben 194
Zimmerman, George 150–151

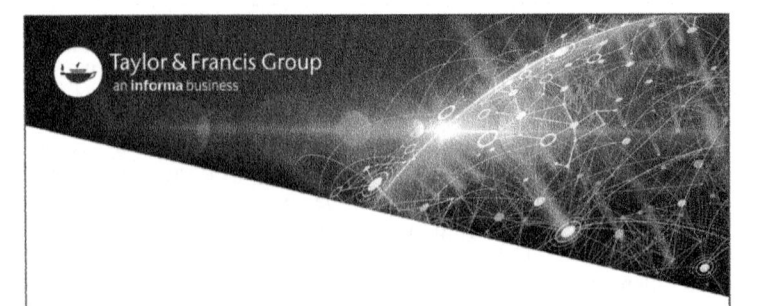

Taylor & Francis eBooks

www.taylorfrancis.com

A single destination for eBooks from Taylor & Francis with increased functionality and an improved user experience to meet the needs of our customers.

90,000+ eBooks of award-winning academic content in Humanities, Social Science, Science, Technology, Engineering, and Medical written by a global network of editors and authors.

TAYLOR & FRANCIS EBOOKS OFFERS:

A streamlined experience for our library customers

A single point of discovery for all of our eBook content

Improved search and discovery of content at both book and chapter level

REQUEST A FREE TRIAL
support@taylorfrancis.com